JUICE NAZI SEEKS HEAD OF SECRET POLICE

guide to running a notorious juice bar

Andrew An Ho

Foodyap

*This book is finished on Alive Juice Bar's tenth year anniversary.
We couldn't have made it this far without our customers.
Thanks to customers who've supported us, especially during
the tough times. You're the best, this book is for you.*

True nostalgia is an ephemeral composition of disjointed memories.

FLORENCE KING

CONTENTS

Title Page
Dedication
Epigraph
Prologue
How it Began
About Alive juice bar
Miranda
Miranda
Miranda
How to Order
...
Living Room
Monkey

Introduction	1
Part I -- Mindset	4
Chapter one -- Sixty rules I learned about owning a business	5
Chapter two -- Mindset of a bad cook	16
Chapter three -- Your hobby is not your passion	23
Chapter four -- So you want to be a porn star?	28
Chapter five -- Ten worst reasons to own a juice bar	33
Chapter six -- Review of Marco Pierre White's memoir, The	36

Devil in the Kitchen: Sex, Pain, and Madne

Chapter seven - Ideas are worthless	41
Chapter eight -- To whom I'd sell Alive Juice Bar	44
Chapter nine -- How the cult of self-esteem produces fuck ups	47
Part II -- Hiring	56
Chapter ten -- Reader reactions to "Juice Nazi Seeks Head of Secret Police" application	57
Chapter eleven -- "Juice Nazi Seeks Head of Secret Police" application	60
Chapter twelve -- Alive Juice Bar is hiring angry people	69
Chapter thirteen -- Alive Juice Bar is hiring very very very nice people	71
Chapter fourteen -- "Seeking Darth(ette) Vadar to Join the Dark Side" application questions	74
Chapter fifteen -- Answer key to application questions	82
Chapter sixteen -- Select application questions explained	97
Chapter seventeen -- Other application questions	105
Part III -- Employees	108
Chapter eighteen -- On human nature	109
Chapter nineteen -- How to spot bullshit	112
Chapter twenty -- Training new employee guidelines	117
Chapter twenty one -- Passage of Seattle's $15hour minimum wage: notes and predictions	120
Chapter twenty two -- The $15/hour minimum wage: bring it on, motherfuckers.	124
Chapter twenty three -- What's a fair wage?	129
Chapter twenty four -- What's a living wage?	132
Chapter twenty five -- Who deserves a "living wage"?	135
Chapter twenty six -- Jobs for all = Dumbfuckingest idea	138

EVER

Chapter twenty seven -- How schools train students to not be responsible	149
Chapter twenty eight -- How to break rules and get away with it	154
Chapter twenty nine -- Alive Juice Bar principles	162
Part IV -- Customers	164
Chapter thirty -- How to talk to customers	165
Chapter thirty one -- Obedient versus responsible	174
Chapter thirty two -- What is means to be responsible	177
Chapter thirty three -- Never say "no" to a customer	181
Chapter thirty four -- How not to run a start up business	184
Chapter thirty five -- Etiquette	191
Part V -- Nuts and bolts	194
Chapter thirty six -- How to run a juice bar	195
Chapter thirty seven -- Use of music	197
Chapter thirty eight -- Guidelines	200
About The Author	205
Praise For Author	207

PROLOGUE

Alive Juice Bar opened in Shoreline WA May 2010. It'll move to Everett in the Fall of 2020.

HOW IT BEGAN

Alive Juice Bar was conceived while we were rafting on the Yamabatutu river, under the shine of a crescent moon, surrounded by dolphins dancing hip-hop moves. Guided by divine providence, we imagined ourselves as Adam and Eve before The Fall. The clothes came off, we threw the snake overboard, and inspiration arrived. We finally felt Alive.

ABOUT ALIVE JUICE BAR

We make the nasty shit taste good. Doing our best to transform ridiculous middle-class habits and sensibilities...one business at a time.

MIRANDA

MIRANDA

MIRANDA

HOW TO ORDER

HOW TO ORDER
(TO HELP KEEP COSTS DOWN)

There are NO lines
Take your time to decide, but
CALL OUT your order the
MOMENT you decide
Wait for someone to confirm
your order. Once confirmed,
relax

FAILURE TO FOLLOW → WILL RESULT IN YOU STANDING AROUND LIKE AN IDIOT.

GUIDELINES
Sometimes the customer is WRONG

LIVING ROOM

MONKEY

XXIX

XXXI

INTRODUCTION

They say the Chinese government is run like a business. The President is the CEO and the Premier is the COO. The Politburo are the board of directors and Communist party members are shareholders. Provincial leaders are district managers and so forth and so on, all the way down to the student interns. Chinese citizens are the customers.

Restaurants -- businesses in general -- are run like the Chinese government. Think Gordon Ramsay. Juice bars, even more so because unlike most restaurants, my job at my juice bar isn't solely to entertain the customer, but also to guide them about matters of health and diet. I don't just cook nutritious drinks and meals that taste good to the customer, I'm expected to nurse sick customers back to health, to prescribe remedies to heal an injury, and to absolve those who've committed dietary debauchery. Which means my job isn't to give customers what they ask for, my job is to build trust. That means I treat customers differently from what you'd get at a typical restaurant. I expect customers to be transparent about what they want and need, and any hint that they're not sets me off.

I might poll customers about their preferences (focus groups) but I don't let them decide what and how I serve because most of them, like American voters (myself included), don't know what the fuck is going on on my end business-wise and on their end health and diet-wise. Want wheatgrass? Go to Jamba Juice, I'm not serving bullshit shots. Want an acai bowl? Go get one at Costco, that shit is a waste of time and resources. The customer isn't always right, the customer is usually wrong, ok? My job is to cut through the bullshit to give my customers not what they want, but what they need to be healthy.

An employee who makes an excuse gets chewed out. No, not later when the customers are gone, immediately because otherwise, they'll forget what happened. Managers run the store as they want as long as we're getting good results, and if the results aren't good, they're fired. There's no states rights or voting. Employee input and checks and balances, sure, we have those in place, just like how it is in China. But no more than that because businesses need to be nimble to survive, we don't have time for long debates and hesitation.

It's not my intention to conflate the Chinese Communist Party (CCP) with the Nazi party, the two parties are nothing alike unless you believe Western -- especially American and British -- media's representations of the CCP and China (I don't). Rather, the "Juice Nazi" moniker that customers gave me references Seinfeld's Soup Nazi, who is based on a real person. In any case, I haven't done anything extraordinary to earn this praise -- I'm not at the same level as great chefs like Marco Pierre White, Jiro Ono, and Charlie Trotter, or great athletes like Tom Brady and Michael Jordan. I'm nowhere as demanding, strict, and disciplined as any of them, which is why I'm nowhere as successful as they are.

My purpose here is to show readers how to run a juice bar without boring those who aren't planning to do so. You can read this book as a behind the scenes reveal of a notorious juice bar, similar to Anthony Bourdain's *Kitchen Confidential*.

This book is divided into five parts and thirty eight chapters. Part I, *Mindset*, shows you my mindset and the reasons for it when I work. Part II, *Hiring*, is a collection of my most controversial application questions and shows how far we go to find the right employee.

Part III, Employees, has musings about human nature -- which you need to understand to run most businesses -- considers how employees should be compensated, and reflects on why the labor market is what it is. Part IV, *Customers*, explains why I treat customers as I do. Part V, *Nuts and Bolts*, shows how Alive Juice Bar is run, from its use of music to attract and repel customers to its batshit crazy way of luring new customers.

This book can be read in whatever order you want. Feedback and questions are welcomed, send it to foodyap@gmail.com. Enjoy!

PART I -- MINDSET

To live is to suffer, to survive is to find some meaning in the suffering.
--Neitzsche

CHAPTER ONE -- SIXTY RULES I LEARNED ABOUT OWNING A BUSINESS

1. It's not fun. Nobody, nothing cooperates. Things break, people are whimsical, weird shit happens all the time.

2. It's a lot of fun. It's fun when you figure out how to cooperate with an unpredictable world. You'll realize the fun is the chase, and the work is in maintaining the relationship.

3. You're a stupid useless cunt every time you fuck up an order. Doesn't matter if this is true or not. You have to believe it's true.

4. Don't hire when you start. I learned this one the hard way and it nearly left me destitute and homeless. It takes time to build a competent army. Hire because you've found the right person, not because you want a break.

5. People don't change, they just become clearer versions of who they really are. Don't expect to change the person you hire into the person you want them to be, even if they want to be that. Our habits are addictions, we relapse when we think we can get away with it.

6. People change only when there's enough peer pressure to do so. That's why she won't lose weight until the flow of compli-

ments about her appearance ends. Until then, she'll see what she can get away with.

7. Never say "no" to a customer. It creates a communication barrier, such that they tune out everything else you say to them. Create a place where customers don't have to hear "no." They already hear "no" all day long, from their boss, their kids, spouse, bureaucrats.

8. If you have to say "no" to a customer, say it without saying "no." For instance, say "Fuck Off." Much more effective than "no."

9. Never make excuses to a customer. Assume that the customer doesn't care if you're late opening the store because your grandmother slipped and broke her hip and you had to take her to the hospital. Just apologize for being late and continue work.

10. Never play victim. Once you start blaming the world for your problems is when it'll soon be over. It's especially important to blame yourself when it's not your fault. Learn to blame yourself when it's not your fault. Only then will you figure out why IT IS your fault.

11. Don't allow employees to play victim. Once they do, it will become a part of the work culture. Making excuses and playing victim are contagious behaviors. We have a policy — three excuses per month and you're fired. Employees can make up for each excuse by writing an essay on why the excuse was made, what will be done to ensure it's never made again, and how making excuses prevents one from learning.

12. "If you are going to kill, kill 20, not just one," someone once told Bandit Queen, Phoolan Devi. "If you kill 20 your fame will spread; if you kill only one, they will hang you." And that's exactly what she did — massacred 22 upper-caste villagers — and that's exactly what happened — pardoned of all crimes after 11 years in jail, elected to office, and immortalized in

books and film as a lower-caste gang leader. Don't just piss off a few people. That's going to happen, unintentionally, anyway. Piss off a lot of people, INTENTIONALLY. Don't piss people off for the sake of pissing them off. That's just douchebag behavior. Piss people off because you truly believe that there's no other option, that they need to be pissed off, that they need a good shake to wake up.

13. It's ok to fail. Most of life is failure. Failure is good as long as you learn from it, take responsibility for your failure. I fail several times a day.

14. Follow the Pareto principle, the 80-20 rule. I had never heard of it until someone mentioned it after noticing that I kept describing the world in 80/20 ratios. This ratio seems to be found throughout nature. Like 20 percent of people own 80 percent of wealth. Or 80 percent of people use 20 percent of software features, while 20 percent use 80 percent of them; 20 percent of agricultural land produces 80 percent of bounty, 20 percent of employees produce 80 percent of value. Fascinating.

15. Hang out with your customers and employees. They're the most important people in your life, they support you even though you're a stupid, useless, cunt. Treat them like family, know them better than anyone else in their life. Don't waste time on those who can't help you reach your goal. There's no time to hang out with college drinking buddies and reminisce about the time the two of you had sex with twins in a bathroom stall while...GROW UP!

16. Operate your business as stereotypical East Asian family operates. If you have no idea what goes on in many East Asian families, read Amy Chua's Battle Hymn of the Tiger Mother. It's an extreme example, but it captures the essence of Asian identity and worldview AND how visionaries like Steve Jobs ran their businesses. She provides a general framework on how to run a business and treat employees. I've tried the standard middle-

class White American way of parenting and it doesn't work. It's like they're in competition to see who can be nicer to their kids and assume their kids are narcissistic, manipulative, and have a strong sense of entitlement because they weren't nice enough to them. It's fucking madness!

17. Don't waste time. Use off hours to identify all the mistakes you made during the day and figure out how to correct them. The mistake could be a posture, choice of words, failure to spot a detail, possibilities are endless. Spend leisure time only on activities related to business. Don't spend time talking to those who don't add value to your life and business. Again, don't waste time. So obvious, but difficult to follow.

18. Be grateful. Thank your customers for putting up with you being a stupid, useless, cunt, for actually paying money for your products and services. Thank your employees for tolerating you. Treat them to lunch and dinner.

19. Don't let customers control the business. It's your business, not theirs. Don't be scared of them. The moment you let them run your business is when you lose passion for whatever it is you want to do.

20. Burn all business textbooks. Some of the stuff you find in textbooks may work for Fortune 500 companies, but not for a start-up. Rely on street-smarts, not books that'll be out of date within 10 years of publication.

21. Ignore consultants. They're mostly talking business textbooks. Their advice is either obvious, asinine, or impractical at the moment. Most of them don't know your motivations. You can learn a lot more from industry veterans.

22. Listen to Tupac, let him guide you, because you will be shot by someone five times and you better "take it and smile." When you recover, find the motherfucker who shot you and destroy him and everyone associated with him. It's better to be feared

than loved.

23. Always compare yourself to the best. Not saying you need to aim to be the best. You don't need to be ambitious (I'm not). But you need to grade yourself fairly. (You need to recognize reality). If you don't like being compared — and we're always being compared, like it or not — find a low stress, low profile, low standards job where comparisons will be implicit, not explicit.

24. Don't get greedy. Realizing expansion is a slow process. I've been tempted to accept free rent to open a second store here and there even though I can barely run one store. A lot of people lose everything when they open a second store or expand. I remember Asteroid Cafe, a little hole in the wall in Wallingford, the owner was passionate about politics. Great reviews, good prices, successful operation for nearly a decade, bursting at seams. Decided to expand, moved to a fancy location in Fremont, tripling seating. Lasted less than two years. Owner crushed, has never recovered. Sad story.

25. Don't be lazy. This is obvious, but it's so tempting to slip up. It's Friday 7pm and you want to go home so you do a sloppy job of interviewing an applicant, cut it short. Her incompetence ends up costing you thousands. Or I once lost a bid for a large catering event because I didn't respond to an email a day earlier. (And even if my late response isn't the reason for rejection, I have to believe that it is. Create a reality that will encourage you to not be lazy).

26. Ignore focus groups. Steve Jobs ignored them. Focus groups are methodologically problematic and people don't know what they want when they're in a contextless environment. They also give you yet another excuse when something doesn't sell. Good sellers can sell anything, even bottled fart. Ann Wigamore convinced people to pay a lot of money for something as useless as wheatgrass.

27. Exercise. You need to be healthy to maximize productivity. You can find the time for it.

28. Don't try to save the world. If your product sounds too good to be true — spirulina, wheatgrass, ionized water — then you are a liar. Stay away from anyone who tells you buying their product will save the world (empower the peasants, save them from greedy capitalists!) and instantly bring you eternal life (wheatgrass). There's no such thing as an elixir. Living well requires hard work. Even then, shit happens. We're no longer in the Garden of Eden.

29. Believe in Original Sin. Especially the Calvinist/Puritan version, where we are born responsible for and tainted by the sins of our ancestors. If you don't believe you're depraved and deserve to burn in Hell, you'll never be truly grateful for life and whatever else you have. You'll feel entitled to a place in the Kingdom of Heaven. You won't have the drive to keep going during the tough times. You won't be able to survive a day where you lose money despite working 16 hours. You have to see the tough days as penance for your sins, not as unfair.

30. Flattery is the sound of the Devil's laughter. Flattery distorts reality, makes us blind to our total depravity. Ignore salespeople who flatter you, they're like the men who flatter women so they can fuck them. Addiction to flattery feeds our narcissism and lowers standards. That's why those at the top rarely praise themselves and other people. Flattery has ruined many promising careers and businesses. Low caliber people work for praise. High caliber people work for achievement. God's people work to express God's grace.

31. Apologize quickly. Apologies disarm. They don't give people a chance to wonder if they were intentionally wronged. Apologies prevent disappointment from lingering or growing into anger.

32. Arguments don't accomplish anything, they're just used for venting. In arguments, it doesn't matter who is right or wrong, most people don't listen to each other. That's why arguments rarely end with someone changing their mind. Arguments end only when one or both parties are exhausted, not because they've reached an agreement. Don't get into arguments with customers about the efficacy of this or that. It's a waste of time to do so.

33. You deserve what you get. When things aren't going well, you deserve it. Never forget your total depravity, your Original Sin, and the sins of your ancestors.

34. When things are going well, you got lucky. Check your ego and narcissism at the door. Never ignore God's grace.

35. Never mistake adulation for love. Love is earned, rarely given. The adulation will end the moment you're not of use to anyone. "Those bastards can take everything away at anytime."

35. Most people don't read. (People like to pretend they do though). Be succinct and use images when communicating with customers.

36. The wordier a person is, the less trustworthy and competent they are, and the more likely they're full of shit and hiding something. The most competent people rarely use softeners when communicating.

37. There's a lot of self-deception out there. Don't try to change it, just work around it.

38. Don't fire employees, make them quit. Less paperwork, less chance of lawsuit. Don't give the Ex a reason to be vindictive.

39. In matters of life and business, follow the heuristic: pick the answer that you think most people won't pick. Put your faith in the Classics of social and political thought, not in cliches and banalities that come and go.

40. You won't' survive if you don't recognize and work with human nature. The Classics are what they are because their take on human nature has been time tested.

41. Think of your business as a school and your employees as students. You're responsible for your employee's futures. Expel employees who don't understand that work is time to learn and grow, not simply time to make money. Focus on placing employees at top businesses, similar to how best schools aim to place their graduates at top colleges or graduate programs. It'll ultimately help you attract talent you need to make your business work.

42. Ideas are worthless. That's why it's ok to let others steal them. Back in the late 80s, analysts thought Starbucks was a dumb idea. Analysts were wrong because they didn't realize that the idea is irrelevant, it's the force of character — Howard Schultz — behind an idea that matters. Invest in character, not in ideas.

43. The character necessary to make an idea worth something is based on a deep sense of insecurity AND superiority. That combination makes confidence.

44. Choose a reality that will encourage you to not be lazy, envious, complacent, or arrogant. If a regular customer stops patronizing your business, don't think it's because they moved away. Assume it's because you did something to ruin the relationship, you didn't meet their standards. I watched a restaurant I invested in collapse because owners chose the wrong reality. They heard that some questioned their taste, so they attempted fine dining to prove them wrong. It was a disaster. It takes extraordinary effort and skill to pull off fine dining. After its collapse, they blamed Seattle for failure, claiming that "Seattle wasn't ready for this kind of sophisticated dining, that it would work if it were in New York City." Bullshit, the Seattle dining scene is very sophisticated. The problem was that they

weren't sophisticated enough for Seattle. Everyone saw that but them. They chose a reality that allowed them to blame others for their failure. Which means they'll never learn from their mistakes.

45. Don't take investor money unless you're certain they'll make money. Be responsible and patient.

46. Your competitor is not your enemy. You need them for brand differentiation. Without them, your customers will always wonder if there's something better and take you for granted. That's why we encourage our customers to try other juice bars.

47. Your employees should fear you. Otherwise they'll take short cuts.

48. Your customers should fear you. Otherwise they'll take advantage of you.

49. Most teachers in the humanities and soft sciences aren't paid to have business sense or to recognize reality. They mostly produce unemployable, bitter people who are dumb enough to believe that the owners of Walmart are willing to pay their CEO millions to do nothing.

50. Make friends with business owners. They share your reality. You'll speak the same language. Not only will hanging out with them be emotionally comforting, they'll teach you something about human nature.

51. It's ok to make generalizations about socially constructed groups. It's important to recognize patterns of behavior among groups of people. It's not ok to reduce an individual to a social identity. That's dehumanizing.

52. Read about the lives and motivations of those at the pinnacle of your profession. (Not saying you need to aim for that pinnacle). They're your mentors, follow their advice on how to

manage staff and customers.

53. Be sure standards are set at level appropriate to your leadership skills and labor pool. Don' t try to be Thomas Keller if you're not willing to put in effort to develop a staff that meets his standards.

54. Customer's perception is your reality. Doesn't matter if the perception is wrong. That's the reality you work with.

55. Sometimes the customer is wrong. Don't let them hurt themselves.

56. The product is secondary. It's more important to control perception of and expectations for the product. For instance, Laughing Ladies Cafe closed because people were turned off by the owner, who has been described on Yelp as an "angry lesbian." Owner didn't need to change her personality to make it work. She just needed to change expectations by renaming the cafe "Angry Ladies Cafe." It would've worked, just as Grouchy Chef, run by a grouchy chef, works.

57. You can get away with being an asshole if you do everything else extremely well. People are willing to put up with difficult personalities if they think they're getting a great deal. Like the Soup Nazi of NYC. Or the Sushi Nazi of Nashville. Or Grouchy Chef of Seattle. NONE of them act as they do because they think they can get away with it. For instance, the Soup Nazi acts as he does out of care and responsibility — he understands that many of his customers have 30 minutes for lunch so he needs the line to move as quickly as possible.

58. Fear, respect, love. In that order. Avoid spending time with those who don't see it this way because they'll fuck you over with their self-deception.

59. Create space and products that are both ahead of and behind its time. People rarely live in the present, they live in the future and past because the present is often painful to them. Give

customers innocence and hope. Create products that will remind them of childhood — simpler times — yet allow them to maintain their adulthood. For instance, our avocado milkshake tastes like a milkshake. But it's green in color, lactose free, and contains kale and collards. It allows the customer to feel like a child and an adult.

60. Make people believe you're crazy and capable of anything, including murder. Have employees spread rumors about you once being charged with murder. Do something crazy but innocuous that gets the police involved. Embellished version of the story will travel fast. Better to be feared than loved.

CHAPTER TWO -- MINDSET OF A BAD COOK

Mindset matters. It's what feeds the bad habits others have written about it.

Bad cooks:

* assume everyone likes what they like.
* take it personally when someone doesn't like what they like
* feel happy when complimented on their cooking
* take it personally when someone doesn't like what they make
* don't consider context
* don't think about what the eater is experiencing
* have high self-esteem

The above explained.

Bad cooks assume everyone likes what they like
Because they're narcissists. It's never occurred to them that other people are not just_like_them, that other people may not want to be treated the way they want to be treated. So they don't make an effort to get to know other people as individuals with their own palates and preferences. Watching them cook is like watching a guy stick his dick up some woman's ass without ever asking her if she'd like that because he assumes every woman likes anal.

Not everyone likes cheesecake. Not everyone likes kimchi. Not everyone likes bacon. Some people like broccoli. Some people like raw oysters. Some people like it up the ass. Some people don't like it up the ass. Bad cooks are like shitty lovers, they're not observant and curious enough — they rarely ask questions — to ever pay attention to their partner's unique preferences.

Just because he likes it up the ass doesn't mean everyone does, ok?

There are only two drinks on my menu that I enjoy and drink daily: the Attitude Cleanse and The Nasty Shit, both of which 99% of people -- some of my customers excepted -- won't like. The drinks I don't drink, they're for customers who have different palate preferences from mine. If I only serve what I like, my business would fail. So know your audience and then figure out how far you'd go to satisfy them. You don't have to take it up the ass if you don't want to. (I've seen juice bars resort to selling alcohol and ice cream to satisfy customers). And don't try to satisfy everyone. If you do, it means you have no integrity. Stand for something.

> **treat other people the way you want to be treated. the most simple rule in life.**

This is a stupid life rule. Narcissists live by this rule because they think that what they want is what everyone else wants or should want.

Bad cooks take it personally when someone doesn't like what they like
"How can you NOT like _____!!!!?????" asks the bad cook. And then he goes on and on and on about how much and why he likes it until he's made it clear to everyone that he's superior to anyone who doesn't like what he likes.

Snobbery doesn't work if the goal is to get someone to like something they don't like. Snobbery is about inflating the ego at another person's expense.

Bad cooks feel happy when complimented on their cooking
Which isn't the same as feeling happy when someone is enjoying food you made. Bad cooks waste their emotions on stupid shit like praise and cook to feed their ego instead of their customers. Put simply, bad cooks are addicted to compliments. Which means they lack integrity, they'll do whatever it takes to get as many compliments as their addiction needs. If there's no purpose to the food other than to win compliments, then sell candy instead of kale because a lot more people want the former than the latter.

And in any case, happiness (or is this contentment?) shouldn't be contingent on external events because you can't control what happens around you and trying to do so is usually futile.

True happiness comes from within, from that faith in oneself to handle any situation with aplomb. Bad cooks are who they are because they're an emotional mess, they lose it when an oven stops working or Gordon Ramsey calls them a "dickface" or a car crashes into their kitchen (which happened to our neighbor, who handled it with humor and nonchalance).

YOU!!
Piss off

Bad cooks take it personally when someone doesn't like what they make
Bad cooks attach their ego to every dish they make. They think working this way makes them "passionate" when in fact it makes them too emotionally needy to ever take risks that make cooking fun in itself. That's why bad cooks stick with popular recipes for popular dishes because it's too risky to invent a dish someone may not like.

Bad cooks don't consider context
Bad cooks are so focused on what they want that they're unable to work with what's available and to cook from multiple perspectives. This limits their repertoire and ability to improvise when something isn't available. It would never occur to a bad cook. for instance, to cook a meal on the engine of a running car (roadtrip cuisine!); to use a lemon instead of a lime to cut cost; to substitute this for when that isn't available; to work with the seasons.

Bad cooks don't think about what the eater is experiencing as they eat
Inexperienced employees often ask what size this apple or that cucumber should be. Never tell or show them the answer. Ask them instead what size the customer wants it to be. What does a woman want to look like while she's eating a salad in public? Does she want to open her mouth as if a porn star is getting ready to swallow some Zulu sized dick or does she want to look dainty? Would customers prefer their bento meals to look half full or almost too full when they open it? How should a salad be arranged to maximize its appeal to customers? How many colors and what type of shapes and textures should be on a plate?

Bad cooks have high self-esteem
They think so highly of themselves that they can't imagine themselves making silly mistakes, like forgetting to put ice in a smoothie. So they never implement checks — eg. feeling the

temperature of the cup after pouring smoothie in it — into their workflow processes, if they even have one.

I AM AWESOME

This hot dog also tastes like shit.

So What Makes a Good Cook?
Good cooks are primarily focused on what their customers want, not what they themselves want. And then they work to strike a compromise between what the customer wants and what they themselves want and are willing to make. What else? Good cooks:

- keep their egos out of their work
- know that they'll make mistakes
- assume everyone has unique preferences

Good cooks keep their egos out of their work
This makes them more objective when assessing their work. This also allows them to not be hurt if someone doesn't like what they make. Which in turn frees them to experiment any way they want because they don't care about rejection.

Good cooks know that they'll make mistakes
That's why they check their work and invite colleagues and customers to check their work.

Good cooks assume everyone has unique preferences
This encourages them to ask customer questions about their

preferences and priorities before telling them what they should get. Good cooks respect each person's individuality.

CHAPTER THREE -- YOUR HOBBY IS NOT YOUR PASSION

Applicants tell me that they'd work "100 hours a week" if they were passionate about their work. Many also tell me that they can't figure out why they lose passion in every interest they pick up. In other words, they're asking me why they're aimless and depressed.

"Give them time, they just need to find their passion," offers the well meaning parent. Cliche aside, sure sure, but how does one find passion? People seem to think it's about sampling as many different interests until there's that — woo woo! — perfect spark, perfect match. Serenfuckingdipity. Those who lack passion simply didn't get a chance to sample enough activities, declares PTA mom who voted to give all students their own laptop. Solution: provide more activities, more electives until every one of these little darlings finds his/her passion.

Won't work because passion is first and foremost an act, not a feeling. If you think it's a feeling that drives action, then you have it ass backwards. It starts as an action — mostly painful and frustrating — that gradually, slowly, leads to a rare euphoric feeling (achievement), to feeling passionate about something. Anything, not just the usual writer-rockstar-journalist-event-planner-jock fantasy. Could be picking up dog shit, or scamming people with three card monty, or pimpin' midget hoes. There's no hierarchy of activities, one can LEARN to be passionate about anything.

Think of it this way, what's the difference between infatuation and love? Infatuation is instant, it's the moment she thinks she's met her ideal man. Let's see: tall (not too) dark (the right kind of dark) and handsome; six figure salary (low six figure so she can maintain her leftie politics without being called a champagne socialist); awww yeah, a nice, Zulu-sized dick (without it coming from Zulu-land). "It was meant to be," she coos. Yeah. Until he demands anal sex from her daily and she develops bowel problems. Zulu dick not so fun now, eh?

Above illustrates what many experience when choosing a calling. The reason why so many lose passion for something — quit — is because they can't handle pain and frustration, failure. They're infatuated with this and that career. They can't take it up the ass because they idealize the life of whatever it is they want to be. They never think about the process of becoming a surgeon; or a rock star; or a porn star; or President of the USA. To develop passion, one must learn to take it up the ass.

Take the kid who wants to be a rock-star. He practices and practices. Sends demos to studios. Only rejections. Dejected, he quits. Another kid keeps going, practices more after each rejection. Keeps going until he gets his first contract. It's disingenuous to say that for the former, it just wasn't meant to be while for the latter, he simply has passion for music. No, the former couldn't handle failure and his feelings of frustration. The latter did. He invested more and more in spite of mounting rejections.

Yeah yeah, there's more to it, we'll discuss later. For now, let's complete the analogy. What do you do to make someone fall in love with you? Jiggling your tits will, at best, get you infatuation, and at worst, have you branded a slut. Seduction means not only making someone notice and want you, but to also work for your affections. And the deeper the investment, the more in love with you he'll be. That's why adage tells women to not spread legs too early, to make the guy wait work work wait for it. You slowly pull him in, show him a bit more of the prize each time he does something right. Push him away when he fucks up. Manipulative? Sure, if you say so. But the other option is a guy who quickly grows bored of you. Or worse, a guy who doesn't grow bored with you because he's boring. Love is earned, rarely given, because love is frustrating work.

The point is, passion, like love, requires work. This work involves mostly lows — rejection and failure — and few highs. The more pain and frustration one experiences, the better the high. The inability to handle rejection and failure — likely due to sense of entitlement and poor impulse control — prevents one from developing passion. I'll ask an applicant, over e-mail:

Hey, thanks for your response. Can you make your responses more readable? Think about how your audience is experiencing your response. Also reconsider your answers for questions 4-9. Do an internet search. Finally, aim to be consistent. Resubmit at your leisure.

Two-thirds respond with a tantrum. Most of the rest respond by trying to do as I ask, treating each task as an annoying hurdle than as a learning experience, dropping out after getting frustrated with being asked to reconsider this and that. Rarely, someone figures out that the interview begins the moment I email them and that they're being tested on how well they handle failure, how they talk about their failures, and their willingness to learn from their failures. I'm testing their capacity for passion.

Why Your Hobby Is Not Your Passion
So you like cooking and serving your friends. Or you can play a video game 16 hours straight. You're starting to think that cooking is your passion. You wonder why a game is so fun but life isn't.

The reason you think cooking is your passion, is pleasurable, is because people compliment you on it. It's fun because your ego is getting massaged. Cooking is not your passion precisely because it's your hobby. Don't confuse the feeling you get from affirmation of the ego (happiness) with passion. Passion rarely feels good. Cooking, for most, isn't so fun when Gordon Ramsay asks you why you're a stupid cunt for frying an egg in boiling oil. If it is fun having a maniac scream in your face about fuck ups your friends and family either won't mention to you or don't notice, then maybe your hobby is your passion.

Video games are fun because they're manipulative. They use push-pull tactics great seducers use to lure their love "victims." They make you struggle, and you're rewarded if you work hard enough, solve enough problems. So why can't this work ethic, this passion to solve problems, be easily carried over to real life? Because real life is REAL, where the consequences of not killing all the Satanic looking giant penguins is REAL death and destruction of humanity. Where a wrong decision means REAL nuclear holocaust. Where serving a bad dish to a REAL prominent reviewer sinks your REAL business. Where "redo" and "restart" aren't options. The pressure is REAL. Most hobbies are NOT REAL. They merely provide ESCAPE from REALity.

How to Train Passion into Child
Say a child wants piano lessons. Make him accomplish something to earn the right to take piano lessons. Don't just give it to him. Make him earn it. He'll be more likely to stick with it if he has to work at getting a shot at it. And when he begins to experience difficulty, DON'T LET HIM QUIT! Don't make the lame excuse of "it's just not his passion," or the equally asinine "it's just not his forte." Don't create someone who will never become passionate about anything. The activity is irrelevant, passion is expressed through one's ability to handle failure and pressure.

Meaning and Fulfillment
Working long and hard isn't enough to make someone passionate about something. The act has to be meaningful. Acts that

are meaningful are those that help other people become better. Any activity can be meaningful. The three card monty scam artist can be passionate about scamming people because he believes he's helping dumbasses figure out how naive and stupid they really are. A beer maker can be passionate about his work because he thinks he's helping people to relax and have a good time with friends. A football player can be passionate about getting brain cells knocked out of him because he wants the feeling of winning a championship and bringing a city together like never before.

The cook who seeks approval and affirmation instead of, say, redefining proper portion sizes to help people control weight is going to hate her job because work, at the highest level at least, is mostly rejection (most people don't like being told they eat too much), little affirmation. The kid who wants to be a rockstar so he can get laid whenever he wants will never become the rock star working to resolve a geopolitical conflict that has cost many lives. Put simply, passion is the act of serving other people. Passion is Sisyphean rage against the inevitable, that "rage, rage against the dying of the light."

CHAPTER FOUR -- SO YOU WANT TO BE A PORN STAR?

Every New Year, new customers ask for advice on opening a juice bar. I'm going to stop telling *nearly* everyone to not do it, to never consider the idea again — Anthony Bourdain and others already shout that message. Do it. Fucking a, DO IT, FOLLOW YOUR PASSION! This for those who want to do it. Fuck Bourdain and other industry insiders for their negative message. They just want to keep the fun for themselves.

Most want to talk about irrelevant shit like recipes ("can I borrow some," "where did you find them," or the more thoughtful "how did you come up with them"). Having the right recipes is the least of your worries. If you're confident in your cooking ability, recipes will come to you serendipitously, the situation will make it happen, just as it has for thousands of years for millions of cooks. If you're asking me about recipes to start a restaurant, I'm thinking you're a daydreamer who is wasting your and my time. Daydreamers ONLY think about results, it never occurs to them to focus on the process — who they have to be, what they have to do — to reach results. When they watch a great performance, they never imagine what it took, the thousands of hours of preparation and practice, the force of character necessary to make the performance happen.

Daydreamers consume, never appreciate, are rarely grateful. Dream builders focus on the process, they understand that the process is the result. The process is the result, the process is the result, even if the result is failure. If you rarely daydream, great. If you do, try to figure out how someone built something you like, whether it be a dish, a menu, a song, a house, a bridge, a personality, whatever. Try to reverse engineer whatever it is you want to build. Consider the motivation of the person(s) who built it. Not only will it get you to stop daydreaming, it'll help you appreciate the world more, help you recognize reality about yourself and other people.

Which brings us to the second point. Asking about the process shows me you're concerned about recognizing reality, reality about yourself and others. Daydreamers don't recognize reality and you can't run a business if you don't see reality. I watched a restaurant I invested in crumble fast because owners couldn't see, refused to acknowledge reality, reality that was clear to all investors and most customers. We pleaded with them to see and work with reality but they refused because it would mean challenging, and ultimately changing, their sense of self. They saw themselves as this and that, which didn't match customer perception. Don't underestimate human self-esteem defense mechanisms. They are powerful enough to allow someone to lose everything rather than confront who one really is.

You want reality? How's this for reality? For a month, make a three egg omelet every morning. Make it in less than a minute. If you can't make a perfect omelet in less than a minute, or if the omelet isn't perfect (runny, slightly burned, contains egg shells), find a mirror. Now stare into your eyes and tell yourself that you're a "stupid, useless cunt." Three times. Because that's what someone is thinking every time you fuck up an order. And even if that isn't true, it NEEDS TO BE TRUE, you have to believe that it's true. If you don't, you'll fail, I guarantee it. "Stupid useless cunt" is what I call myself every morning. Makes my piss smell good, helps me piss straight. If you can't handle treating yourself this way, you're not going to last a month owning and running an unbranded restaurant.

So you're starting to or always have been able to see reality and you can deal with it. Here's another dose of reality. Reality is that you're a stupid, useless cunt and very few, if anyone, love you. You think x,y,z love you, whatever the fuck "love you" means? They likely don't love you, they need you. Maybe they need your money. Or they need your skills as a wingman. Or your praise and flattery to confirm their (un) reality. Don't confuse need with love (and I believe love exists, but is never, ever cheaply and easily attained or given). The sooner you realize that there's very little love in the world — in spite of non-stop declarations to the contrary — and the sooner you understand that people are much more responsive to fear than to declarations of love, the sooner you'll discover reality and be able to make lemonade out of it. Machiavelli was right, the hippies are wrong, it's better to be feared than loved, especially in a world where love is commodified, cheap, almost meaningless. Fear, not love, makes the world go round. Think about why the 1984 commercial introducing the Apple Macintosh is so iconic. The plot:

Gray industrial setting, hot female athlete is chased by four scary looking police officers armed with large night sticks. She races towards a large screen with the image of a Big Brother-like figure giving a speech about the benefits of a one world government. The runner, now close to the screen, hurls the hammer towards it, right at the moment Big Brother announces, "we shall prevail!" In a flurry of light and smoke, the screen is destroyed, leaving the audience in shock.

This commercial is effective because it exploits people's fears, fears about their future and their identity. It takes advantage of American obsession with individuality. It's telling you that if you don't pay attention to the Macintosh, we'll turn into an Orwellian society, no more freedom. The message isn't "Apple loves you please buy the Mac" because people don't respond to love. The message is "you need the Mac if you want to be who you think you are or want to become" because people respond to fear, in this case, fear of losing one's identity and so-called freedom.

Once you understand that few, if any, love you, and that it's better to be feared than loved, you'll either commit suicide or be able to get to work on making a lot of people to not only need you, but maybe even, if you're really special, a few to love you. You'll be able to devote yourself to thinking about the wants and needs of others. You may be able to figure out what they really want, not what they think they want. You'll realize that love is earned, rarely given.

If you think I'm being cynical, if you're not convinced that fear, and not love, makes the world go round, read Bourdain's Medium Raw, which offers many short bios of chefs, including an entire chapter devoted to David Chang. Also read the bio of Marco Pierre White, Devil In the Kitchen. Understand what drives the best chefs, what makes them tick, how they think. Often, it's not love of cooking, that's just a symptom, a manifestation of a deeper psychological crisis. More often, at the core, it's fear, hate, rage, shame, fear, fear, rage, fear. A sick, twisted addiction to confronting fear, to beating it, often with rage. Why do you think David Chang, whom Bourdain considers the "most important chef in America" "hates you?" Not saying you have to be just like a crazy Marco Pierre White mofo to open a juice bar. I'm a mellow dude (stop laughing, I am!) and I don't intend to win any Micheline stars or even a pat on the back. But you need to know what it takes — mindset and attitude — to reach the pinnacle of a profession if you want to survive in that profession. You need role models to pull you in the right direction. Because if you think it's about smiling and being nice and friendly, you'll be crushed. Not saying assholes always finish first. Not saying your name has to be "Fuck You" to make it work. Am saying that nice people are too petty, innocuous, and unoriginal to survive this (or any other) game. Nice people sit so they don't get hurt. Being nice is easy. Being responsible isn't (but is a lot more rewarding). That's reality. Ask yourself if you're willing to be a part of reality.

If you're comfortable with reality, we'll talk about the nitty gritty. Like supply chain and inventory management, human resources, workflow processes. Maybe we'll talk recipes. At times, I'll remind you that just because you love cooking — currently one of the trendiest hobbies — and serving food and all your friends tell you you're good at it doesn't mean you should turn your hobby into a business. I mean, just because you like sex and have a big cock or nice breastesses and a few people have told you you're good at it doesn't mean you should become a porn star. You really think it's that easy to get your cock up when *they* want it up? You really think it's that easy to make 12 kale salads in five minutes while handling four drink orders and have enough charm to keep everyone laughing and entertained?

And if you go through with it, remember that you'll be paid and respected like a porn star. Because in the end, unlike with engineers or mathematicians or surgeons, you do what most people can and in fact do, cook. The only difference is that you get paid to do what you do, you can get your cock up when *they* want it up and you cum when *they* want you to. Most of the time, or enough so they don't fire you. Are you still horny?

CHAPTER FIVE -- TEN WORST REASONS TO OWN A JUICE BAR

10. You want to be your own boss. No you don't. Most people don't. I don't. Most people are followers, want to be led, told what to do. I allow myself 20 minutes of fantasy time per day and I spend half of it imagining being someone's bitch, being told what to do. I even put a craigslist ad out seeking someone to be my boss.

9. You want to make a lot of money instead of being exploited. The money can be good. But keep in mind that business owners don't get a minimum wage or union protection or tenure. You'd be completely exposed to an unpredictable world, such as a pandemic that cripples your business. As Marco Pierre White put it, "those bastards can come knocking at any time and take it all away."

8. You want to run a business the "right" way. You're going to show Walmart/McDonald's/greedyevilbusinessoftheday how it should be done. You're going to pay everyone really well and be really really nice to them so they work really really really hard and you'll all get really really really really rich together it'll be a big happy family. If it were that easy, we wouldn't need God. There'd be heaven on earth. Not saying you can't run a business your way. I've broken many business textbook rules. Just saying it's not easy to pull off.

7. You want to be passionate about your job. So you want to turn your hobby into your job, and you're convinced you'll do well if you finally pursue something you enjoy. No. Your hobby — cooking — is fun because it isn't your job, you're not graded on it by strangers and colleagues day in, day out. It's a hobby because there's no pressure to do well or else. It's a hobby because for most, it's an escape from reality and pressures of life.

6. You think you'll care more if it's your business. No you won't. How much you care, your work ethic, depends on habit, not if it's yours or not. If you're doing a shitty job at someone else's job right now, you'll most likely do the same shitty job working on your own business. You won't be able to care about your business until you learn to care about someone else's business.

5. You want to work less. I need to pee.

4. You think you have a great idea/product. But ideas are worthless. It's the force of character behind an idea that matters.

3. You think you have great recipes, you're convinced grandma's meatloaf recipe will make you a million bucks. Most recipes are worthless in a restaurant environment. In fact, they're often dangerous, can sink a restaurant because they're so complicated. And it's not that easy to develop a menu. A menu is not a collection of your greatest hits. A menu is designed to support workflow processes and is based on utilities infrastructure. That's why we rarely accept recipes from well meaning customers. Most don't know how to hedge risk or how to work with the infrastructure.

2. You think it'd be glamorous. Actually, it is, in some ways. Be sure you enjoy being under a microscope. I had no idea people would care so much about this or that about my life, that I'd be a source of neighborhood gossip. If you're an extravert, you may enjoy the attention. If you're like me, an intensely private extreme introvert whose idea of fun is playing chess against a

computer, you'll find it emotionally draining.

1. You want to serve God, deliver God's will and message. Actually, this is the only good reason to open a juice bar or a restaurant. This reason will give you the stamina and discipline to keep going during the toughest times. This reason will significantly reduce probability of you fucking everything up in your own fucked up way.

CHAPTER SIX -- REVIEW OF MARCO PIERRE WHITE'S MEMOIR, THE DEVIL IN THE KITCHEN: SEX, PAIN, AND MADNESS

Chapter One. Marco Pierre White, when his maitre d' fucks up a cheese plate:

I picked up the first cheese. "Not right!" With all my might I threw it against the wall. It stuck to the tiles. I picked up the second cheese "Not right! I chucked it at the wall. Then I hurled the remaining cheese, one after another, at that wall.

Nicolas and a couple of cooks raced over to the wall, ready to pry off the cheese and clear up the smelly mess. I shouted, "Leave them there. Leave them there. Leave them fucking there all night. No one is allowed to touch them." The cheese had to stay on that wall all night so that whenever Nicolas came into the kitchen, he would see them glued to the white tiles and would never, ever make the mistake again.

What makes a great cook, who becomes a great chef? What drives someone to work 17 hour days, 6 days a week? Marco Pierre White's memoir, Devil in the Kitchen: Sex, Pain, and Madness answers these questions. Read it if you want to be a better cook. Read it if you want a career in the restaurant industry. Read it if you're stupid enough to consider quitting your well paying job to pursue your "dream" of owning a restaurant. Read it if you want to enter the mind of the Devil. Read it if you want to be the Devil.

White is considered the first postmodern "rock star chef," and the youngest ever, at age 33, to win three Micheline stars. He's Big Daddy O, a big fucking deal. We owe him (and Japanese food shows) the Food Network (otherwise we'd be stuck with Julia Child version 4.0 and Giada's tits). He trained some of the guys we watch on TV: Gordon Ramsay (White claims to be the only person to break him); Mario Batali (quit after White threw hot risotto at him); Curtis Stone; Heston Blumenthal, the list goes on. Lots of Micheline stars. So how does he do it? His words:

You have to deliver the message that they must never take a shortcut. You can't just say, "Come on, boys, let's try to get it right." That just won't work. If you are not extreme, then people will take shortcuts because they don't fear you. And to achieve and retain the very highest standards, day after day, meal after meal, in an environment as difficult and fast as a restaurant kitchen, is extreme, well, in the extreme.

Put simply: Fear, Respect, Love. In that order.

Fear
White is a master at instilling fear because he's able to enter people's spirit. He has extraordinary observation skills. White biographer Bill Buford notes that though White dropped out of school at 16 — he was labeled a dumbass because of his dyslexia — and has always had difficulty reading, he found that White comprehends everything that's read to him:"genius level comprehension ability." What separates White from the mediocre is that he pays attention, and is able to do so for long stretches. White is thus able to learn faster and to get to know people

more deeply. He's able to enter another's spirit, understand what another perceives.

Here's a rough Buford example of how White enters the spirit of an employee. White will ask him about his family, past, hopes, aspirations. From that he figures out his fears. Here's how it goes down when this employee makes excuses or complains (some artistic license):

White: *I knew you're going to be just like your father, you fucking cunt. You're going to beat your wife just as your father beat your mother. You're going to beat your children just as he beat you. You're going to be another drunk, useless, cunt. Stand in that corner.*

But psychological terror and humiliation (he really did make employees stand in the corner, even ran out of corners once) wasn't enough. He used the threat of physical punishment to cement their fear. He turned off the AC when employees complained about the heat. He cut up the shirt and pants of an employee who complained about the heat. He threw all sorts of stuff at people, including hot risotto at Mario Batali.

Most didn't last a week in White's kitchen. But enough stayed and some of them, like Gordon Ramsay, became great chefs.

Respect
White earned respect of employees, customers, and reviewers because he didn't let any of them fuck with him. Employees respected him because he was quick to eject pain in the ass customers. Customers respected him because his employees had his back, always ready to brawl. Reviewers respected him because he didn't give a shit what they thought — returned all his Micheline stars and told them to fuck off. He stuck to his convictions and learned to not let employees, customers, and reviewers run his business. He believed in himself. He stood for something.

Love

"Those bastards can come any day and take it all away." White doesn't count on anyone to love him and resists the urge to mistake adulation for love. That's why he never lets his guard down and is always trying to improve. White also understands love as an act, not as a feeling. "Every man should build a monument to his mother" (his mum died when he was 6). For White, words of love are meaningless. There must be proof, and the proof is in the monument.

While Devil in the Kitchen is primarily a story about how White reached the pinnacle of his profession, throughout there are snippets of advice for amateur cooks. Not recipes, he's primarily interested in teaching the proper mindset and methods. White, on the cook's brain:

Cook's brain. It's that ability to visualize the food on the plate, as a picture in the mind, and then work backwards. There's no reason why domestic cooks can' do the same thing. Cooking is easy: you've just got to think about what you are doing and why you are doing it.

Apply the cook's brain and visualize that fried egg on the plate. Do you want it to be burned around the edges? Do you want to see craters on the egg white? Should the yolk look as if you'd need a hammer to break into it? The answer to all these questions should be no. Yet the majority of people still crack an egg and drop it into searingly hot oil and continue to cook it on high heat. You need to insert earplugs to reduce the horrific volume of the sizzle. And the result, once served up in a pool of oil, is an inedible destruction of that greatest ingredient — the egg. Maybe that's how you like it, in which case carry on serving your disgusting food.

This is the kind of advice that amateur and professional cooks need to improve results. For White, cooking isn't about following recipes. Cooking is reverse engineering whatever it is one wants. It's about entering another person's spirit — understanding how someone experiences what you make for them. It's about serving and pleasing other people, never the affirmation of one's ego.

CHAPTER SEVEN - IDEAS ARE WORTHLESS

When someone asks me to comment on an idea, I *used* to usually tell them that it sucks. I now realize it doesn't matter what I or anyone else thinks about the idea. Nor does it matter if it turns out that the idea isn't as original as one thinks (if you've thought of it, good chance many others have thought of it before you), and that every execution of that idea has resulted in failure. Ideas are worthless. It's the force of character behind an idea that matters. An idea's value isn't dependent on market demand, it's dependent on one's ability to create and control demand.

Most people think that successful businesses are made because they were built on great ideas. Wrong, it's the other way around. The most successful businesses are made because someone *made* an idea great. Consider Starbucks. Most analysts thought Howard Schultz idea of elevating average American taste in coffee and having them pay five bucks for it every day was a terrible idea, a yuppie fad that wouldn't last, a habit that would never be picked up by the masses. They were wrong because they didn't understand that the idea is irrelevant, that trends and consumer habits are mostly controlled by a select few who have the force of character to do so. It's stupid to invest in something just because you like the idea — I've done that before and it rarely turns out well. Invest in character, not in ideas.

Invest in YOUR character, not in get-rich-quick schemes.

When you tell someone their idea sucks, do you mean to say that you don't think enough people will like whatever it is that person wants to sell to them? Or are you saying that this person doesn't have what it takes to execute the idea? If it's the former, then you're limiting yourself, you don't live in a world of endless possibilities, you don't understand yourself or other people, you probably waste a lot of time brainstorming with people as clueless as you, you're a slave to other people. If it's the latter, then you either understand that ideas are worthless and it's the character behind them that matters or you're projecting your shortcomings. If you think most ideas are great (esp. from those you like), then you're fucking wasted, you're too nice and have nothing to contribute. Go back to bed.

Bottled fart, ram penis hotdogs, midget porn, fresh raw juice at people's doorsteps every morning, let's keep it all in play. Anything is possible, there are no bad ideas, stop worrying about market demand. The moment you become obsessed with market demand is when you become a slave to other people. Better to recognize that we're all deeply flawed characters. Instead of asking people if you have a good idea or not, ask *the right people* if you have the character to execute the idea. Ask yourself if you have what it takes — habits, mindset, attitude — to get the job done. Figure out what it takes to get the job done. No, not the technical expertise, I'm talking about the force of character who can manage the unexpected and execute an idea.

Someone recently asked me about a business idea — providing customers with fresh juice at their doorsteps every morning. I resisted the urge to tell her that it's a bad idea. (It *feels* like a bad idea to me only because I don't think I have the force of character to make such a business successful, but this isn't about me, it's about her). I instead tried to get to know her, her work habits, where she's from, what she's experienced. She, on the other hand, wanted me to share my technical expertise and didn't understand why I asked so many questions about her character. It didn't take long to figure out that she doesn't have the force of character to execute the idea. She really believed she could run this business, teach yoga, and attend grad school at the same time. She's had a history of being a dilettante. She seemed incredulous that it would require 100 hours a week of her time, that she's getting herself into some serious shit the moment she signs a lease and has overhead bills to pay.

I bet her friends have told her that she has a great idea, that they'd love to have fresh juice delivered to their doorsteps every morning. I'm confident that none of them asked her about her character. The lack of introspection is why it was so easy for her to become passionate about the result — fresh juice to everyone — but not the process — the force of character — it takes to achieve the result. That's why I prayed to God that evening to have mercy on her, to give her clarity of thought when it's time to sign the lease.

CHAPTER EIGHT -- TO WHOM I'D SELL ALIVE JUICE BAR

I'm not going to sell it to anyone. I'm going to sell it to someone who can grow and continue to express core values of the business. I don't want to come in and find shit like wheatgrass being sold for five bucks and I'll continue to expect employees to be intense and focused, not bubbly and fake. I just want a different personality and mindset to run the business, a gentler, softer presence, someone who can refine established practices and products. I want Alive Juice Bar to evolve. New products, better processes, more effective outreach.

By "gentler, softer," I don't mean nicer. This is a business — no minimum wage, no union protection, no tenure for the owner — business owners don't have the luxury to be nice. Being nice is easy, it's lazy, it's one step above acting like a douchebag, and that's why there's so much of it in the world, so much that it's a cheap commodity. Being nice is not the same as being responsible, compassionate, patient, kind, and understanding.

Put it this way. Pretend you're a teacher. What would you do after an earthquake big enough to topple a few bookshelves? Nobody is hurt, everyone is okay, just jittery. What do you, as a teacher, do?

a) Stop class, act jittery and anxious because that's how you feel.
b) Have students clean up mess and continue class as if nothing

happened. Assign double the amount of homework and quizzes for the rest of the week.
c) Stop class, bring in a school psychologist to discuss how everyone is handling the event and "post-traumatic stress disorder."

If you picked A, you're self-absorbed. If you picked C, you're nice. If you picked B, you'd do what famed math teacher Jaime Escalante did in real life (and he asked that a psychologist NOT visit any of his students to discuss the event). Escalante was able to get students at his poor inner city high school to pass the AP Calc exam at rates unheard of except at the best schools. His "dynasty," as he called it, crumbled after he left. You think it was because his replacement wasn't nice enough? Who do you think is more responsible, the "nice" teacher worried about the amount of pressure placed on kids or the tough one who works them harder than they've ever worked? Which teacher works harder to ensure students have a good future?

As a parent (imagine yourself as one if you don't have kids), what would you prefer to do if your child isn't able to play, after an hour of practice, two bars of a piece assigned by a piano teacher?

a) Congratulate her for trying her best. Give her ice cream and watch her favorite movie with her.
b) Make her keep practicing until she gets it right. No dinner or breaks until she gets it right. Stay up with her until she gets it right, even if it means an all-nighter
c) Tell your kid it's not her fault she can't get it right. Ask piano teacher to assign easier pieces.

The real life mom who picked B has a daughter who played solo at Carnegie Hall at age 14 and is an undergrad at Harvard. Who is the more patient, loving mom? Love is an action, not a feeling. That's the primary message of I Corinthians 13. And if it is a feeling, it ought to be painful and exhilarating.

Look at those at the top of their professions. Bill Parcells publicly humiliates his players. Bobby Knight grabs and screams at them. Barack Obama believes in the Bobby Knight school of training and his White House basketball games are reportedly vicious. Michael Jordan puts anyone who doesn't meet his standards down. Everyone is a "fucking" something or another to Hillary Clinton. Steve Jobs explodes, calls his employees "Fucking Dickless Assholes" when they can't meet a deadline. Marissa Mayer is in your face for this and that. Marco Pierre White will throw hot risoto at an employee who complains. White's apprentice, Gordon Ramsay…just watch one of his shows.

Not saying the Buyer has to act like any of these maniacs. We're not trying to win any Micheline stars. I especially don't want anyone to throw anything hot or sharp at my employees. Just want the business to thrive and to do so, the Buyer has to know what it takes to run one well. If you find the behavior of those at the top of their professions troubling, then you're not cut out to run a restaurant. If they inspire you, if you want to work for them, then running a restaurant is the right job for you. Let's talk.

By "gentler, softer," I mean someone with a subtle but effective presence. Someone who leads by example. Someone unassuming. The person most people don't notice until there's a crisis, which is when this person takes over and shows his/her mettle. Someone who won't yell at customers who walk in with a Frappuccino. Someone who will play fewer songs about death. Someone who won't charge a customer a dollar to change the music.

CHAPTER NINE -- HOW THE CULT OF SELF-ESTEEM PRODUCES FUCK UPS

A professional model, not quite a supermodel but aspires to become one, dumps her boyfriend. He's a good guy, has a good job, is good looking. Cock is large enough, he's just kinky enough, no premature ejack issues. Cool parents and siblings, no douchebag friends, no troubling mental health issues. Sort of a guy who gets women to battle royale each other.

Why did she dump him? Pick:

a) He criticized her looks too often.
b) He complimented her looks too often.
c) She's an arrogant, narcissistic bitch.

Think about it. We'll get back to this later. Open a bottle if you're nervous. I'm probably already ahead of you. Cheers.

Quotes from those most consider supremely confident and successful

Will Smith: "I still doubt myself every single day. What people believe is my self-confidence is actually my reaction to fear."

John Lennon: "Part of me suspects that I'm a loser, and the other part of me thinks I'm God Almighty."

Meryl Streep: "You think, 'Why would anyone want to see me again in a movie?' And I don't know how to act anyway, so why am I doing this?"

Maya Angelou: "I have written eleven books, but each time I think, 'Uh oh, they're going to find out now. I've run a game on everybody, and they're going to find me out.'"

"Whaaaat," some are thinking. What's with the low self-esteem? "How can…if I were…" Hold that thought. And don't project, other people are NOT you and you're not them.

Defining self-esteem and self-confidence

Don't confuse self-esteem with self-confidence, even if too many psychologists conflate the two. If you do, you won't be able to understand what's going on above. Self-esteem is one's PERCEPTION and ASSESSMENT of oneself, eg. I'm smart, I'm good looking, I'm a dumbass, I'm repulsive. Self-confidence is one's FAITH in one's ability to achieve something, eg. I'll hit 50 home runs, I can make the cover of Vogue, I can beat the shit out of that motherfucker, I'll find the cure to cancer.

Prevailing assumption is that one must have high self-esteem in order to have high self-confidence. One must think highly of oneself — "I'm brilliant! — in order to find the cure for cancer. Concomitant assumption is that those with low self-esteem will be failures and are prone to violence, drug abuse, etc. Such assumptions make it tempting to conflate self-esteem with self-confidence.

Self-esteem is rooted in one's perception of one's environment. An All-State basketball player who didn't receive D-I scholarship offers may consider himself not very good at basketball because he compares himself to D-I players. The best basketball player on a last place high school team may consider himself a great basketball player because he only compares himself to his teammates.

Self-confidence is primarily built on achievement in a competitive environment. Like the MVP of the NBA. Perfect MCAT scores. An Academy Award. The more objective the assessment of one's ability, the higher its value and impact on confidence level. (Academy Award, for instance, is partially a subjective assessment of ability).

The Self-Esteem movement

Some claim Ayn Rand's boytoy, Nathaniel Branden (of all people), started the self-esteem movement back in 1969. Whatever, who cares. Point is, the theory that one must have high self-esteem in order to have the confidence to achieve socially acceptable goals began to gain currency in academic circles sometime around that year. Theory mostly circulates in the academy for a decade, where it's refined, debated, and pushed (and tested) on eager and impressionable undergrads. Some who, ten years after graduation, began to wield socio-cultural influence, perhaps as journalists, teachers, PTA moms.

Who was listening? Champagne socialists aside, it's those who looked up to college grads. That is, those who didn't go to college but wanted so badly their kids to do so. They thought they were getting the inside scoop on how to get ahead even though it would've worked out better if their son had taken over a plumbing business that pays $120,000 a year instead of getting a bullshit degree from a bullshit college. Cult of self-esteem grows as Oprah and Glamour mainstream the feel good message to the aspirational working and middle-class by growing and feeding their narcissism. Different sorts of narcissism, as Machiavellianism is so passe in post-industrial America. This is narcissism by repression, projection, and ironic contradiction. Kids are taught to repress fundamental emotions such as fear and anger. Feeling hate? Project project project, "it's not me, it's him, I'm all love," rationalizes the kid robbed of his lunch money. And what better way to bolster the ego than community service? "I am special and should be admired because today, I volunteered my time to help people," she thinks as she rolls a spliff and begins four hours worth of daydreaming about her glamorous future and picking up as many "Likes" on Facebook as she needs to feel good about herself.

Tenets of Self-Esteem Movement

1. Be nice. Don't hurt anyone's feelings.
2. Focus on what one's good at instead of struggling with the unfamiliar.
3. Everyone is special, everyone is a winner
4. You can do and become whatever you want. Whatever you want (echo-o-o-o).
5. Avoid stress and pressure to maximize performance.
6. When stressed or hurt, talk about your feelings.

How the narcissist understands these tenets:

1. Don't hurt my feelings by pointing out my fuck ups. And I'll do the same for you. Deal?
2. I'm allowed to avoid reality, to not think about my fuck ups and how to fix them.
3. I should avoid situations that make me look like a loser.
4. Let me daydream and delay the inevitable realization that there are limits and achievement requires extraordinary time and effort, for which I'm not prepared.
5. Heaven on Earth is possible, the blissful life. It's ok to live life as a series of escapes.
6. It's socially acceptable to live inside one's head, and to not be responsible for one's feelings.

Self-Esteem and the bizarre

A teenage boy comes in. His parents are the types who continually remind him that "you can do whatever you want, you can be whatever you want." Places order. I begin small talk. He's a big boy so I ask: "you play football?" His response: "Nah. Football coach thinks it's a waste of my physical attributes. But whatever. I can do whatever I want. I can do whatever I want."

Ok. I understand. Kumar (of Harold and Kumar) points out that just because one has a big dick doesn't mean one should become a porn star. That's fine, I get it. Then it gets weird.

"What sports do you do?"

"Track."

"Which events?"

"Pole vault."

"Aren't you kinda big for that?"

He has three options. He can tell me that I'm wrong, that he has the ideal body for such an event and explain why that's the case; or I'm right and he's an outlier. Third option is what he chose: "I can do whatever I want, man. I can do whatever I want."

Someone tell me that I'm not the only one with the urge to knock this kid out cold and lock him in a dungeon until Stockholm Syndrome sets in for life. This was a bizarre and scary exchange. Total disregard of what's best for the team. Completely focused on what the self wants. Imagine his future:

Detective: Why did you think it was ok to forcibly stick your cock in that girl's mouth?

Boy: I can do whatever I want, I can do whatever I want.

Detective: I bet you can. And Uncle Shirley can do whatever he wants, whenever he wants too. I can't wait for you to meet him.

What kids hear

Parent says: You can be whatever you want.
Kid hears: I will be seen as squandering my special talents and powers if I don't achieve greatness. I'm not prepared for this kind of pressure. I need to start searching for excuses.

Parent says: You can do whatever you want.
Kids hears: Who cares about the wants and needs of others.

Parent says: You did a great job, great effort kiddo.
Kids hears: Not really, but I guess I'll take it. Thanks.

Kids who are talked to in this way are more likely to become envious, narcissistic adults who need non-stop praise and affirmation to stave off depression and anxiety. Alternatives:

Parent: You can reach your goals if you put in appropriate amount of time and effort.
Kid hears: I'm responsible for my achievements. I decide my place in society.

Parent: You're free to make your own mistakes. Learn from them.
Kid hears: There are consequences to every one of my actions and I'm responsible for them.

Parents: You need to work on that more if you want to get better.
Kid hears: I'm not that good, but I can get better.

First kid will think he's great and KNOWs he's not that good. Second kid thinks he sucks but KNOWS he can do better. Big difference. Beginning to see how someone as accomplished as Will Smith can act confident yet be so insecure? First kid will make excuses when he fails or only hang out with acolytes who praise him, feeding him bullshit bullshit bullshit so he grows up to rely on bullshit sandwiches (compliment followed by criticism followed by compliment) to get through work. Second kid will seek criticism, and screw the praise, that's a waste of time. There are standards to meet, visions to realize, and that's all that matters in life.

"I tried my best, I did and gave everything I could," parents tell me. No you did not. I was there, I saw it. I watched you fuck up your kid in your own fucked up way — the needless coddling, the glib praise, the undeserved gifts, the lame excuses, the anxious cheers. You're not a cheerleader, you're a parent, you're the coach. So parent and coach. Cheerleaders cheer, coaches teach and berate and motivate. Watch how the best coaches treat their players. Jim Calhoun, Bobby Knight, Jim Harbaugh: these motherfuckers scared the shit out of their kids and every single one of them is better for it. That's how you're supposed to treat your kids. That's how you win a championship.

Why is the self-esteem movement so attractive?

It promises great results with little work. Takes effort to qualify a loaded statement like "you can be whatever you want." Takes even more effort to put such a statement in action: showing them what it takes, how it's done, by putting in the work yourself. Takes extraordinary effort to stay up with them through the night as they practice practice practice until your eyes are bloodshot and they get it right. Stop telling them how much you love them — that's a cop out — love requires ACTION, love is an act, not a feeling. Words are meaningless, people want acts of love, not bromides. No wonder glib slogans are more appealing. Allows parents to feign work and deflect blame when their kids turn into fuck ups.

The self-esteem movement promises Heaven on Earth. As with all attempts at making utopia happen on earth, the consequences are disastrous. Studies are showing: more violence, more depression, more envy, more anxiety, not less. Less achievement, less happiness, less self-confidence, less motivation, not more. Good news is that the Atlantic Monthly reading and NPR listening demographic has figured this out because their media sources have been telling them "reverse course reverse course we fucked up" for the past 10 years (see Atlantic Monthly on Cult of Self-Esteem, google it). But how long will it take for the Cosmo and People mag reading demo to figure it out? Is it too late for them and their progeny, are they destined to a lifetime of bullshit sandwiches?

What makes people go batshit crazy?

People go crazy when their sense of self is at odds with other people's perceptions of themselves. Bridget thinks she's gorgeous. Because all her friends tell her so on Facebook. Mom and Dad too. Now lock her in a building full of Vogue cover models and make Anna Wintour (real-life Devil Meets Prada) her boss. Let's see if she can last two months. She either emerges batshit crazy or a better person.

Put differently, dissonance between self-esteem and "reality" makes someone batshit crazy. That's why the person who thinks he's "oh so smart" avoids putting himself in situations that'll make him look stupid. Or the person who thinks she's funny and never notices that she's the only one laughing at her self-described "sarcastic wit" (whatever is being taught in English class, just stop stop stop it) will never have the courage to do stand-up on comedy night. People seek spaces and people who confirm their sense of self, their identity. And tend to avoid those who challenge their self-esteem. It's no wonder that those who invite and give criticism are the executives, while those who can't take it are managed staff, fed a steady diet of bullshit sandwiches to keep their fragile sense of self intact.

How to treat a model

Let's return to the model who dumps her boyfriend. Which response did you pick?

I think she dumped him because he complimented her looks too often. Guys, if you want to date a model, NEVER tell them how gorgeous they are. And not because she hears it all the time from those whose standards she disregards. Think about it, why did she become a model? Because she's tall and gorgeous? Plenty of women out there like that who don't become models, or try and fail. No, she became a model because she was insecure about her looks during her teen years. Perhaps schoolmates made fun of her lanky frame, hollowed cheeks, and buggy eyes. She grew accustomed to the criticism, desired it because it confirms her sense of reality, that she's not good looking. As she grew up and filled out and became what most consider beautiful, she stopped getting the criticism she desired. That's why she became a *successful* model, so some gay guy can pinch her thighs and tell her how fat and ugly she is, so she can be surrounded by people better than her. Her job confirms her reality. Her boyfriend didn't. So she dumped him and went to work.

Supermodels are supermodels because they're never satisfied with their looks, NOT because they think they're gorgeous.

When parents give their kids a reality — Heaven on Earth — that will never exist, they're giving pharma drug companies a few more customers. Kids can live their unreality for only so long before they're forced to accept that Santa doesn't exist; Lassie will die; Grandma is the tooth fairy; Grandpa watches barely legal porn; Mom's fucking her trainer; Dad sucked boyfriend's dick. That she's not as smart, pretty, and funny as she and her friends and family think she is. The ones prepared for reality will be able to change it. Those unprepared will be left confused, helpless, and crushed. That's reality.

PART II -- HIRING

The first method for estimating the intelligence of a ruler is to look at the men he has around him
-Machiavelli

CHAPTER TEN -- READER REACTIONS TO "JUICE NAZI SEEKS HEAD OF SECRET POLICE" APPLICATION

HATE MAIL

"Hi, I just wanted to let you know that your tag line in your craigslist ad is the most deplorable thing i've ever seen a business put their name on.
I've taken photos of the ad, with the name Alive Juice bar right under the bottom of the photos on your ad, and I will be posting them on social media"

"…what kind of employee do you expect to attract with an application that is as crude as yours?"

"I can handle all kinds of bullshit, but that application was offensive. Maybe I don't want my kid to feel pressure to grow up to have a nine inch cock and girlfriend to ride it. Maybe I want my kid to grow up being emotionally and intellectually well adjusted, maybe even gay. That preferred answer denotes an immense level of heteronormativity and even a budding trend towards misogyny."

"…this "application" takes methods of communication to a

whole other level. How does your business remain open with an application like this being online?"

"...the Asian references are pretty tasteless. But you are forgiven."

"Is this a real ad? If it is, I'm shocked"

"Wow. Just wow."

(Facebook)
"He's like an annoying Midwestern morning radio host who doesn't even get paid anymore, just wants to jack off into the microphone and call it "edgy".

(Facebook)
"Alive is a racist cult built around the shitty, awkward personality of someone who thinks trolling is a business model."

LOVE MAIL

"Best damn Blog i ever read and interview I have ever taken. I will happily be your minion and enforce your will on all who oppose you."

"Omg hahahabbabab!
I read your ad,
I love you!
I love you."

"I wanted to share how inspiring your post has just been as I continue looking for work, I would answer C to all the questions. Because, why would I ever dull the life around me with idle lack of accountability or good taste (relatively). My shit is as together as it can be working on less than consistent stability or responsible nourishment to my body. I am strong, now at 22 I realize while climbing out of my adolescent intercity self victimization, radical self love and the ability to laugh in place of tears has burned brightly in the fog of codependency, unhealthy expectations, and post traumatic stress disorder. Its much more funny in hindsight I have decided. Either way cheers for the post, I needed this. Ciao!"

CHAPTER ELEVEN -- "JUICE NAZI SEEKS HEAD OF SECRET POLICE" APPLICATION

Taking applications for January 2018 start. Full or part-time. Manager position $15-18/hour plus tips. Staff position is $11.50-$14/hour plus tips.

More of a Continental European style service than stupid suburban American style. Meaning, don't hide incompetence behind fake smiles and vacant small talk. Get shit done right.

Apply if you want to learn how to:

* Hack open a coconut with a badass butcher knife
* Stop whining about stupid shit
* Stop making lame excuses
* Call a customer a Fuck-Face when asked to do so
* Make kale and yam chips
* Give memorable great service
* Give will-be-remembered-on-death-bed shitty service
* Learn to ask good questions
* Not tolerate middle-class manners and sensibilities
* Stop talking like a pompous fucktard
* Listen and comprehend
* Make juices and smoothies from scratch

*Write a resume and cover letter

Perks: free drinks, some free food. Free dance classes in our dance studio, free use of dance studio during off peak hours. Field trips to cool restaurants so you learn about interesting food. Mostly regular customers. A lot of good looking customers. Interesting customers too because we've ejected most of the shitheads.

Boldface answers. Send to Foodyap@gmail.com. Some questions can have two correct answers.

1. What should a Mother say to get her son to eat something he doesn't want to eat?
a. Drink that kale smoothie or I'll kick your ass.
b. Drink that kale smoothie if you want to grow a nine inch cock and find a girlfriend who'll ride it.
c. Baby, drink that kale smoothie, it's good for you, do it for mommy, ok?

2. Daughter wants a car. How should she ask her parents?
a. I got straight As, I deserve a car.
b. Mom, buy me a car or I'm telling Dad you've been fucking Uncle Burt.
c. If you buy me a car, I'll drive you home when you get wasted, like you do every weekend. It'll cost less than a DUI lawyer and increased insurance rate.

3. A woman most consider beautiful thinks of herself as ugly. Which comment makes her feel best?
a. You're gorgeous.
b. You need to lose some weight.
c. Anyone who thinks you're ugly is an idiot.

4. Which 6 year old is most likely to become a serial killer?
a. The one who gets bitch slapped for getting a B
b. The one who tortures animals for fun.
c. The boy who is forced to dress like a girl by his sisters.

5. Customer walks in (you don't know his name). How do you greet him?
a) Hey!
b) Hello sir, how are you this evening?
c) Wussup, fuckface?

6. The bus shows up 10 minutes late, making you 10 minutes late to work. Whose fault is it that you're late?
a) Bus driver's
b) Traffic's
c) My fault

7. Customer greets you with: "Hi, how are you?" How do you respond?
a) I'm doing very well. How are you?
b) What do you want?
c) I'm making rice and beans. Try some!

8. An employee leaves sharp knives in soapy water. What should you say to her?
a. Please don't do that again, it's dangerous, someone can get hurt.
b. If you're sadistic and want to see blood, fine. If not, you're a self-absorbed knucklehead.
c. Do that again and I'll kill you with the knife I find in the water.

9. You get called to Principle's office because your daughter told teacher to shove her stupid lesson, which you also think is stupid, up her ass. What do you do?
a. Ground her, tell her rude behavior is never tolerated.
b. Reward her
c. Defend her, tell principle she's been struggling with mental health issues.

10. Your kid gets caught selling drugs in school. What do you do?
a. Ground her, tell her she'll ruin her life if she keeps doing this

b. Send her to military school
c. Don't do anything

11. Earthquake during math class! Big enough to topple bookshelves. Nobody is hurt, everyone is okay, just jittery. What do you, as a teacher, do?
a) Stop class, act jittery and anxious because that's how you feel.
b) Have students clean up mess and continue class as if nothing happened. Assign double the amount of homework and quizzes for the rest of the week.
c) Stop class, bring in a school psychologist to discuss how everyone is handling the event and "post-traumatic stress disorder."

12. Pick best sentence:
a) Would you mind bringing me some beets when you get a chance?
b) Get beets now.
c) Hey fucktard, get your ass over there, get some beets and bring it over here.

13. Salesperson calls, asks "Hi, how are you doing today?" How do you respond?
a) What do you want?
b) I'm fine. How are you today?
c) I feel like shit. I want to beat the shit out of someone.

14. Pick best sentence for love-text:
a) Your scintillatingly luminous presence inspires and captivates my yearning heart to take an unsolicited leap of impossible faith into the great unknown of the comfort of your arms.
b) My darling, my heart aches for your presence and to finally be in your arms
c) Let's cuddle.

15. Pick best sentence for first sentence of novel:
a) Dreary black skies loomed as the violent waves crashed onto glittering rocks that have never met such punishment.

b) It was a dark and stormy night; the rain fell in torrents — except at occasional intervals, when it was checked by a violent gust of wind which swept up the streets.
c) Fucking hurricane knocking down trees.

16. Technician finally calls you back. He asks: Hi, how are you doing today?" How do you respond?
a) I'm fine, how are you today?
b) How do I fix this problem?
c) This problem is driving me crazy. Because of your fucked up system, I can't get my kids to school on-time, my cat took a dump on my pillow, and my husband is a lazy piece of shit who wants a divorce.

17. What do you work for?
a) Praise and reward
b) A sense of achievement
c) To express God's will and grace

18. Mary's daughter is throwing ice cubes at other customers. What do you do?
a) Tell them to "get the fuck out."
b) Politely ask Cassie to tell her daughter to stop
c) Throw ice cubes at them.

19. You're the principal of the school. You visit a class where students are either goofing off or sleeping. What do you do?
a) Tell everyone that anyone who doesn't pay attention will get a failing grade for the day.
b) Don't do anything. Privately tell the teacher that he sucks at teaching, that's why nobody is listening.
c) Explain to students why it's important for them to pay attention to their teachers.

20. You're sampling drinks. What do you say to get sqmeone to try one?
a) "Hi, would you like to try this?
b) "Try this."

c) "Drink this or I'll hit you."

21. What happens when a school district gives middle-class high school students their own laptops?
a) Playing field is leveled, they perform almost as well as those rich privileged kids at elite private schools like Lakeside.
b) They watch porn and play games on laptop while in school, no change in academic performance.
c) They perform worse, laptops make people stupid.

22. What effect does raising teacher wages have on teacher performance?
a) They don't perform any better or worse, people are creatures of habit
b) They perform better, money is a great motivator
c) They perform worse, money corrupts.

23. Who will most likely grow up to be batshit crazy?
a. Asian kid who gets bitch slapped for getting a "B" because "B" is for Bitch.
b. Black kid molested by his football coach
c. Middle-class White kid who gets to do whatever she wants, whenever she wants.

24. Someone leaves knives in soapy water. What do you do to make sure that person never does it again?
a) Tell her that doing that can hurt someone, that she needs to think about the consequences of her actions.
b) Lock her in the freezer for an hour.
c) Fill the sink with soapy water and knives. Have her wash knives.

25. Your 8 year old is new at school. He gets shoved out of the lunch line and is told to get to the back. He responds by beating the shit out of the kid who bullied him. What's your response?
a) Ground him and make him apologize to the kid he beat up.
b) Tell him he did the right thing and to never worry about lawsuits, you'll take care of those if they come up.

c) Have your kid apologize to the kid he beat up and have them talk it out. End with hug.

26. Your daughter loves gymnastics and is about to enter her first meet. She's confident about winning and even thought about the perfect place to hang her blue ribbon. While she did well, she didn't medal, and was devastated. What do you, as a parent, tell her?
a) Tell her you thought she was the best
b) Tell her she has the ability and will surely win next time.
c) Tell her she doesn't deserve to win because she didn't work hard enough.

27. You move to a new school district and your son, who was a B and C student, is now a straight A student. What do you do?
a) Send him to another school, this school must suck
b) Congratulate and reward him for working so hard
c) Tell him this school is a lot better, previous school sucked.

28. Your co-worker moved something to the wrong place and you know it's in the wrong place. Manager asks why it's in the wrong place. How do you respond?
a) She put it there, not me.
b) I don't know, no idea how it got there.
c) I'll move it.

29. Owner teaches you to make something one way. Manager teaches you to do it another way. You're working with the manager, owner is watching. Whose way do you follow?
a) Manager's
b) Owner's
c) Do your own thing, show them you're a superstar!

30. Jane walks in and orders two 32 oz jars of juice, which will take you 15 minutes to make. Jared walks in immediately after she places her order and orders a small juice, which takes 2 minutes to make. Sam enters immediately after Jared places his

order and orders a smoothie, which takes 30 seconds to make, whom do you serve first?
a) Jane
b) Jared
c) Sam

31. Customer who doesn't know what to order asks you what your favorite drink is. How do you respond?
a) Tell him your favorite drink
b) Ask him which flavors he prefers
c) Tell him you'll tell him if he tips you $10.

32. You notice someone checking out your ass as you're making a drink. What should you do?
a) Continue as usual
b) Tell him to stop because it's making you uncomfortable.
c) Wiggle it.

33. Your car battery dies so you're late for work. Whose fault is it you're late?
a) Nobody, sometimes shit happens
b) The battery's.
c) My fault

34. A customer asks you what's the most popular drink. How do you respond?
a) Tell him what you think is most popular.
b) Ask him which flavors he prefers.
c) Ask the manager to answer his question.

35. How do you produce kids who will become confident adults with healthy self-esteem?
a) Tell them how amazing, wonderful and special they are.
b) Set higher and higher expectations and expect them to achieve them.
c) Try to build a stress free environment for them so they can achieve their goals.

36. How do you produce kids who will become batshit crazy as adults?
a) Tell them how wonderful and special they are, all the time.
b) Beat the shit out of them
c) Ignore them

37. How do you improve academic performance at a school?
a) Increase funding so facilities can be improved.
b) Increase number of (real) Asian students
c) Increase salaries so teachers perform better

38. You're the principal of the school. You visit a class where students are either goofing off or sleeping. What do you do?
a) Tell everyone that anyone who doesn't pay attention will get a failing grade for the day.
b) Don't do anything. Privately tell the teacher that he sucks at teaching, that's why nobody is listening.
c) Explain to students why it's important for them to pay attention to their teachers.

39. Who is most likely batshit crazy?
a. Tiffany
b. Olga
c. Phuc-Dat

40. Who is most likely suicidal?
a. Carmela, she's a prostitute
b. Jimmy, he's a social justice activist
c. Tyrone, he's in jail

CHAPTER TWELVE -- ALIVE JUICE BAR IS HIRING ANGRY PEOPLE

One full-time manager; one assistant manager; one part-time barista's bitch;

Manager job duties: prep food and drinks with precision and alacrity; change expletive laden music when kids walk in; serve customers; listen — learn about and from — customers; tell customer to fuck off; remind customers to shut bathroom door; figure out what people really want, not what they say and/think they want; recognize patterns of behavior; deal with hungover and emotional co-workers; berate customer for acting like an asshole; ask questions; draw stuff on windows; download music; clean mess; correct co-worker's grammar; explain why ionized water is for dumbasses; explain difference between glycemic load and glycemic index so customers stop freaking out about carrot juice; tell customer it's ok to stare at your ass but be discreet about it; ask customer if he has a small dick; ask customer if she has a big dick; kick customer who grabs your ass; make inappropriate comments that will get you fired everywhere except at Microsoft; make co-worker stop acting like a whiny bitch; babysit your Bitch.

Assistant Manager duties: same as Manager's but needs Manager permission to tell customer to fuck off and to download music.

Barista's Bitch job duties: shut-up, observe, learn, emulate, ask questions. Cry at home.

Seeking someone who *preferably* (not necessarily):
*Has road rage issues
*Speaks foreign language(s), esp. Russian, Vietnamese, Korean, Ukrainian, Redneck, whatever
*Can swear in foreign language
*Likes hacking things
*Adds hot sauce to everything
*Has kicked someone, hard
*Has been kicked, hard
*Doesn't have nutrition degree
*Dropped out of high school
*If college, major ing/ed in Math or Science or Philosophy
*Can hit a ball
*Has been humiliated
*Can catch ball
*Looks pissed
*Looks mean
*Looks flirty
*Looks ashamed
*Looks kind
*Looks aggressive
*Looks like a Juice Bar employee/customer

If you don't research Alive Juice Bar (or any other business you apply to) on Yelp, you deserve to wipe your ass with maple leaves for the rest of your life.

Attach resume. Keep the cover letter short, don't bore us. Just tell us what we need to know.

CHAPTER THIRTEEN -- ALIVE JUICE BAR IS HIRING VERY VERY VERY NICE PEOPLE

Alright, motherhuggers, since the last ad — Alive Juice Bar Hiring Angry People — was flagged within 14 hours of its posting (new record by 10 hours) by, ironically, some really angry foul-mouthed people, we're going to try a new approach. Instead of seeking "angry people," we're going to try to attract "nice people." And no more swearing. This is a civilized operation.

Manager job description: prep food and drinks at one's own pace; have employees do the same at their own pace; play music from Norah Jones and Diana Krall entire shift; smile at customers; keep smiling at customers as they tell you their order; even bigger smile if you need to ask them to repeat what they ordered because you were so busy smiling, you didn't listen to what they were saying; shut bathroom door when customer doesn't; pick up whatever customer throws on the ground instead of in the garbage can; keep smiling; give diabetic customer extra extra extra sugar because that's what he asks for; maintain smile; hug hung-over and emotional co-workers; ask as nicely as possible (with big big smile) for customer to stop kid from throwing ice cubes at other customers; offer kid ice cream to stop him from throwing things at customers; initiate time-out for group hug when an employee gets stressed during lunch rush; call police when guy makes you or employee uncomfortable; call police when customer asks employee where she got her jeans (and other such sexually inappropriate questions); call police when customer pinches employee ass; ensure employees use proper words when addressing someone of color; make sure employees do not describe customers with racial or ethnic descriptions; initiate group hug at the end of each shift; ask employees how they are feeling at least once an hour; maintain ratio of 200 praises to 1 criticism.

Barista job description: do as manager tells you to do. Smile more often than does Manager.

Barista's Assistant job description: Do as Barista tells you to do. Smile at all times.

Seeking nice person who:

* Starts every sentence with a compliment
* Can say "hello," and "thank-you." in at least 3 foreign languages
* Has never scratched, slapped, or bitten someone during sex
* Doesn't like it when dogs sniff each other's butts because that's dirty
* Considers a neutered dog humping another neutered dog rape
* Addresses customers as "Maam" or "Sir."
* Spends at least 2 hours a day complimenting people on Facebook
* Never gets angry, regardless of situation
* Smiles all the time
* Sounds like that teacher from South Park when asking for something
* Can listen to R Kelly's "I Believe I can Fly" all day long without going crazy
* Holds hands behind back while standing
* Holds hands in front while standing
* Never puts hands on hips and rarely uses hand gestures

* Does not honk when car in front is idle at green light
* Drives safely by merging onto highway at 40 miles an hour
* Looks happy
* Looks agreeable
* Looks friendly
* Looks beta
* Looks doe eyed
* Looks naive

CHAPTER FOURTEEN -- "SEEKING DARTH(ETTE) VADAR TO JOIN THE DARK SIDE" APPLICATION QUESTIONS

The Jedi code is stupid. The Dark Side is the right side. We will teach you the ways of the Dark Side. The Sith code:

Peace is a lie, there is only passion.
Through passion, I gain strength.
Through strength, I gain power.
Through power, I gain victory.
Through victory, my chains are broken.
The Force shall free me.

Job Description: Enforce our will on all who oppose us. Keep proto-fascists out of Death Star. Do whatever it takes to grow and defend the Empire.

Job Perks: free juice, some free food. Free use of dance studio when it's not being used.

Below are our application questions. Your answers will show us if you're ready to join the Dark Side and what you need to learn to harness the Dark Force. Boldface your answers, like this:

Which color ball do you prefer?
a) This one
b) That one
c) This is a stupid question.

Send with resume to foodyap@gmail.com

---

1. Whom does Chewbacca want to bang?
a) Princess Leia
b) C3PO
c) Darth Vader

2. Who has the biggest penis?
a) Yoda
b) Darth Vader
c) Chewbaccca

3. Pick best Golden Rule:
a) Treat others as you want to be treated
b) Treat others as they treat you
c) Trick or treat!

4. Pick:
a) Love, Respect, Love
b) Fear, Respect, Love
c) Love, Goose, Love

5. Do you believe in self-love?
a) No, only those who are chronically unhappy and deeply troubled believe and need that shit.
b) Yes, in this time of hate, we all need to love ourselves more so we can love others more.
c) No, that's not allowed in Death Star, which I've sworn to protect.

6. Why are you so smart?

a) I'm not smart, only stupid people think they're smart
b) I've always worked hard and set the highest standards for myself. I took the most challenging courses and tasks and wouldn't accept anything less than an "A" at school and at work.
c) I'm naturally smart, it's God given.

7. How often do you screw up?
a) Rarely, and when I do, it's someone else's fault.
b) Never.
c) All the time, I'm such a fuck up..

8. Why are you so lazy?
a) I daydream a lot.
b) I'm not lazy.
c) I make excuses and blame others when something goes wrong..

9. Why are you so stupid?
a) I don't know what I don't know.
b) For the last time, I'm not stupid, I'm brilliant!
c) I've got to be if I'm filling this out..

10. What's Plato's Republic about?
a) Why we're all dumbasses
b) The meaning of life
c) How to be happy

11. How many hours a week does the CEO of Walmart work?
a) 100
b) 70
c) 40

12. How many hours a week does Eminem work?
a) 100
b) 70
c) 40

13. How many hours a week does 50 Cent work?

a) 100
b) 70
c) 40

14. How many hours a week does Taylor Swift work?
a) 100
b) 70
c) 40

15. What is Taylor Swift most likely doing right now?
a) Shaving off tied up Luke Skywalker's pubic hair with his light saber while singing Blank Space
b) Singing Teardrops on My Guitar while having sex with Anakin Skywalker as a tied up Padme watches
c) Doing take after take for her next video

16. What was Eminem likely doing on random date, 2003?
a) Getting high and smacking his hoes
b) Working alone in recording studio, repeating same three lines over and over again because he demands perfection from himself.
c) Getting his dick licked by two of his dancers.

17. What does the CEO of Walmart do all day?
a) Figures out new ways to exploit hard workers like me.
b) Sets strategy and vision, negotiates partnerships, builds company culture, and manages supply chains to ensure consumers get what they want when they want it.
c) Pretending he's Jabba the Hut while banging his secretary dressed as Princess Leia

18. What was Tupac Shakur most likely doing during a typical evening?
a) Reading Machiavelli's The Prince.
b) Drinking his 40 and smacking his hoes like they're ewoks.
c) Having a threesome and some cocaine.

19. What was 50 Cent doing on a random Saturday night, 2006?
a) Getting fucked up his ass by his trainer, who resembles Han Solo
b) Working out, writing songs and negotiating business contracts.
c) Sucking your mom's big black dick, what the fuck does this have to do with the Dark Side?

20. Pick best sentence for first sentence of novel:
a) Dreary black skies loomed as the violent waves crashed onto glittering rocks that have never met such punishment.
b) It was a dark and stormy night; the rain fell in torrents — except at occasional intervals, when it was checked by a violent gust of wind which swept up the streets.
c) Fucking hurricane knocking down trees.

21. Ten young women on a trip to a faraway land and stopped and robbed. Five are picked to be raped. What do you think the 5 NOT PICKED are thinking?
a) Whew, at least I wasn't raped!
b) I feel terrible for those who were raped.
c) Am I ugly?

22. How do you produce kids who will become batshit crazy as adults?
a) Tell them how wonderful and special they are, all the time.
b) Beat the shit out of them
c) Ignore them

23. Why are you so lazy?
a) I don't have many responsibilities
b) I'm not lazy, I give it my best every day.
c) It's too hard to think about the wants and needs of others.

24. What would you most likely pay money to watch?
a) Rabbit humping a growling cat
b) Tchaikovsky's Nutcracker Suite

c) Guy sucking his own dick.

25. What percentage of businesses fail within 5 years?
a) 50 percent
b) 20 percent
c) 2 percent

26. Are business owners entitled to a living wage?
a) Yes, everyone is entitled to a living wage.
b) No, it's business owner's fault she sucks at work and life
c) No, but we should set up programs to help business owners succeed.

27. Your partner tells you you're lazy. How do you respond?
a) Takes on to know one, asshole.
b) How am I lazy?
c) You never see all the things I do for you.

28. OPEN ENDED QUESTION
Person A from age 5 to 25, attends school 6 hours a day, studies 4 hours a day, spends 6 hours of leisure time learning to build and building, with like-minded friends, random things, like a tree house, a bridge, a dog walking robot. A also spends an hour per day daydreaming of building something that will improve world's standard of living. At age 25, he graduates with a Masters degree in electrical engineering and is offered a salary of $150,000 to work as a product developer for a green tech company. He gets 3 weeks vacation, full benefits. He accepts the position and works 60-80 hours per week, and is expected to be available for phone calls and e-mails during his vacations. He pays Federal Government 30 percent of his earnings.

Person B, from age 5-25, attends school 6 hours a day, studies 1 hour a day, spends 6 hours of leisure time passively watching TV shows and films like Jersey Shore and Twilight, 3 hours a day daydreaming about being wealthy and pampered and adored by everyone. At age 25, he graduates with a degree in Basic Bitch and a minor in Socks, Drugs, and Rock and Roll. Unable to find a job in his field of study, he takes a job as a cashier at McDonald's, making $12 per hour, 40 hours per week, or $24,000 a year. He doesn't have to pay taxes.

Let's assume one of them is "underpaid." Which one and why? (One sentence, keep it short).

29.. Pick best Golden Rule II
a) Treat others as you want to be treated.
b) Treat others as they want to be treated
c) Treat others as they treat others

Why are you so emotionally fragile?
a) My parents coddle and make excuses for me
b) I didn't have enough traumatic experiences during childhood.
c) I'm not fragile, I'm strong and brave! Smart and hard-working too!!!

31. Someone mugs you. Whose fault is it that you got mugged?
a) My fault
b) Society's
c) Mugger's

32. How many years SHOULD you spend in jail?
a) 0
b) 1-3
c) more than 3

33. OPEN ENDED QUESTION
Mary hires Peter and Paul to dig two ditches, assigning one to each. Peter finishes in one hour because he used his latest invention, the super-duper soil remover zapper. Paul, using a shovel, finishes his in 8 hours. How much should Mary pay Peter. How much to Paul? Whom should she hire if she wants a third ditch?

34. How many hours did Peter spend developing his latest invention, the super-duper soil remover zapper?
a) 2, genius comes naturally to him

b) 200, he got a lucky break
c) 2000, innovation is hard work

35. Who is most likely to grow up batshit crazy?
a. Kid living in Syrian war zone
b. Middle-class White kid
c. Bill Gates's kids

36. The person who wrote this application:
a) Is an angry motherfucker.
b) Is batshit crazy. This is some fucked up shit.
c) Is trying to be funny. Ha ha. Ha. Right?

CHAPTER FIFTEEN -- ANSWER KEY TO APPLICATION QUESTIONS

1. What should a Mother say to get her son to eat something he doesn't want to eat?
a. Drink that kale smoothie or I'll kick your ass.
b. Drink that kale smoothie if you want to grow a nine inch cock and find a girlfriend who'll ride it.
c. Baby, drink that kale smoothie, it's good for you, do it for mommy, ok?

2. Daughter wants a car. How should she ask her parents?
a. I got straight As, I deserve a car.
b. Mom, buy me a car or I'm telling Dad you've been fucking Uncle Burt.
c. If you buy me a car, I'll drive you home when you get wasted, like you do every weekend. It'll cost less than a DUI lawyer and increased insurance rate.

3. A woman most consider beautiful thinks of herself as ugly. Which comment makes her feel best?
a. You're gorgeous.
b. You need to lose some weight.
c. Anyone who thinks you're ugly is an idiot.

4. Which 6 year old is most likely to become a serial killer?
a. The one who gets bitch slapped for getting a B
b. The one who tortures animals for fun.
c. The boy who is forced to dress like a girl by his sisters.

5. Customer walks in (you don't know his name). How do you greet him?
a) Hey!
b) Hello sir, how are you this evening?
c) Wussup, fuckface?

6. The bus shows up 10 minutes late, making you 10 minutes late to work. Whose fault is it that you're late?
a) Bus driver's
b) Traffic's
c) My fault

7. Customer greets you with: "Hi, how are you?" How do you respond?
a) I'm doing very well. How are you?
b) What do you want?
c) I'm making rice and beans. Try some!

8. An employee leaves sharp knives in soapy water. What should you say to her?
a. Please don't do that again, it's dangerous, someone can get hurt.
b. If you're sadistic and want to see blood, fine. If not, you're a self-absorbed knucklehead.
c. Do that again and I'll kill you with the knife I find in the water.

9. You get called to Principle's office because your daughter told teacher to shove her stupid lesson, which you also think is stupid, up her ass. What do you do?
a. Ground her, tell her rude behavior is never tolerated.
b. Reward her
c. Defend her, tell principle she's been struggling with mental

health issues.

10. Your kid gets caught selling drugs in school. What do you do?
a. Ground her, tell her she'll ruin her life if she keeps doing this
b. Send her to military school
c. Don't do anything

11. Earthquake during math class! Big enough to topple bookshelves. Nobody is hurt, everyone is okay, just jittery. What do you, as a teacher, do?
a) Stop class, act jittery and anxious because that's how you feel.
b) Have students clean up mess and continue class as if nothing happened. Assign double the amount of homework and quizzes for the rest of the week.
c) Stop class, bring in a school psychologist to discuss how everyone is handling the event and "post-traumatic stress disorder."

12. Pick best sentence:
a) Would you mind bringing me some beets when you get a chance?
b) Get beets now.
c) Hey fucktard, get your ass over there, get some beets and bring it over here.

13. Salesperson calls, asks "Hi, how are you doing today?" How do you respond?
a) What do you want?
b) I'm fine. How are you today?
c) I feel like shit. I want to beat the shit out of someone.

14. Pick best sentence for love-text:
a) Your scintillatingly luminous presence inspires and captivates my yearning heart to take an unsolicited leap of impossible faith into the great unknown of the comfort of your arms.
b) My darling, my heart aches for your presence and to finally be in your arms

c) Let's cuddle.

15. Pick best sentence for first sentence of novel:
a) Dreary black skies loomed as the violent waves crashed onto glittering rocks that have never met such punishment.
b) It was a dark and stormy night; the rain fell in torrents — except at occasional intervals, when it was checked by a violent gust of wind which swept up the streets.
c) Fucking hurricane knocking down trees.

16. Technician finally calls you back. He asks: Hi, how are you doing today?" How do you respond?
a) I'm fine, how are you today?
b) How do I fix this problem?
c) This problem is driving me crazy. Because of your fucked up system, I can't get my kids to school on-time, my cat took a dump on my pillow, and my husband is a lazy piece of shit who wants a divorce.

17. What do you work for?
a) Praise and reward
b) A sense of achievement
c) To express God's will and grace

18. Mary's daughter is throwing ice cubes at other customers. What do you do?
a) Tell them to "get the fuck out."
b) Politely ask Cassie to tell her daughter to stop
c) Throw ice cubes at them.

19. You're the principal of the school. You visit a class where students are either goofing off or sleeping. What do you do?
a) Tell everyone that anyone who doesn't pay attention will get a failing grade for the day.
b) Don't do anything. Privately tell the teacher that he sucks at teaching, that's why nobody is listening.
c) Explain to students why it's important for them to pay attention to their teachers.

20. You're sampling drinks. What do you say to get someone to try one?
a) "Hi, would you like to try this?"
b) "Try this."
c) "Drink this or I'll hit you."

21. What happens when a school district gives middle-class high school students their own laptops?
a) Playing field is leveled, they perform almost as well as those rich privileged kids at elite private schools like Lakeside.
b) They watch porn and play games on laptop while in school, no change in academic performance.
c) They perform worse, laptops make people stupid.

22. What effect does raising teacher wages have on teacher performance?
a) They don't perform any better or worse, people are creatures of habit
b) They perform better, money is a great motivator
c) They perform worse, money corrupts.

23. Who will most likely grow up to be batshit crazy?
a. Asian kid who gets bitch slapped for getting a "B" because "B" is for Bitch.
b. Black kid molested by his football coach
c. Middle-class White kid who gets to do whatever she wants, whenever she wants.

24. Someone leaves knives in soapy water. What do you do to make sure that person never does it again?
a) Tell her that doing that can hurt someone, that she needs to think about the consequences of her actions.
b) Lock her in the freezer for an hour.
c) Fill the sink with soapy water and knives. Have her wash knives.

25. Your 8 year old is new at school. He gets shoved out of the

lunch line and is told to get to the back. He responds by beating the shit out of the kid who bullied him. What's your response?
a) Ground him and make him apologize to the kid he beat up.
b) Tell him he did the right thing and to never worry about lawsuits, you'll take care of those if they come up.
c) Have your kid apologize to the kid he beat up and have them talk it out. End with hug.

26. Your daughter loves gymnastics and is about to enter her first meet. She's confident about winning and even thought about the perfect place to hang her blue ribbon. While she did well, she didn't medal, and was devastated. What do you, as a parent, tell her?
a) Tell her you thought she was the best
b) Tell her she has the ability and will surely win next time.
c) Tell her she doesn't deserve to win because she didn't work hard enough.

27. You move to a new school district and your son, who was a B and C student, is now a straight A student. What do you do?
a) Send him to another school, this school must suck
b) Congratulate and reward him for working so hard
c) Tell him this school is a lot better, previous school sucked.

28. Your co-worker moved something to the wrong place and you know it's in the wrong place. Manager asks why it's in the wrong place. How do you respond?
a) She put it there, not me.
b) I don't know, no idea how it got there.
c) I'll move it.

29. Owner teaches you to make something one way. Manager teaches you to do it another way. You're working with the manager, owner is watching. Whose way do you follow?
a) Manager's
b) Owner's
c) Do your own thing, show them you're a superstar!

30. Jane walks in and orders two 32 oz jars of juice, which will take you 15 minutes to make. Jared walks in immediately after she places her order and orders a small juice, which takes 2 minutes to make. Sam enters immediately after Jared places his order and orders a smoothie, which takes 30 seconds to make, whom do you serve first?
a) Jane
b) Jared
c) Sam

31. Customer who doesn't know what to order asks you what your favorite drink is. How do you respond?
a) Tell him your favorite drink
b) Ask him which flavors he prefers
c) Tell him you'll tell him if he tips you $10.

32. You notice someone checking out your ass as you're making a drink. What should you do?
a) Continue as usual
b) Tell him to stop because it's making you uncomfortable.
c) Wiggle it.

33. Your car battery dies so you're late for work. Whose fault is it you're late?
a) Nobody's, sometimes shit happens
b) The battery's.
c) My fault

34. A customer asks you what's the most popular drink. How do you respond?
a) Tell him what you think is most popular.
b) Ask him which flavors he prefers.
c) Ask the manager to answer his question.

35. How do you produce kids who will become confident adults with healthy self-esteem?
a) Tell them how amazing, wonderful and special they are.

b) **Set higher and higher expectations and expect them to achieve them.**
c) Try to build a stress free environment for them so they can achieve their goals.

36. How do you produce kids who will become batshit crazy as adults?
a) **Tell them how wonderful and special they are, all the time.**
b) Beat the shit out of them
c) Ignore them

37. How do you improve academic performance at a school?
a) Increase funding so facilities can be improved.
b) **Increase number of (real) Asian students**
c) Increase salaries so teachers perform better

38. You're the principal of the school. You visit a class where students are either goofing off or sleeping. What do you do?
a) Tell everyone that anyone who doesn't pay attention will get a failing grade for the day.
b) **Don't do anything. Privately tell the teacher that he sucks at teaching, that's why nobody is listening.**
c) Explain to students why it's important for them to pay attention to their teachers.

39. Who is most likely batshit crazy?
a. **Tiffany**
b. Olga
c. Phuc-Dat

40. Who is most likely suicidal?
a. Carmela, she's a prostitute
b. **Jimmy, he's a social justice activist**
c. Tyrone, he's in jail

1. Whom does Chewbacca want to bang?
a) **Princess Leia**
b) C3PO

c) Darth Vader

2. Who has the biggest penis?
a) Yoda
b) Darth Vader
c) Chewbaccca

3. Pick best Golden Rule:
a) Treat others as you want to be treated
b) Treat others as they treat you
c) Trick or treat!

4. Pick:
a) Love, Respect, Love
b) Fear, Respect, Love
c) Love, Goose, Love

5. Do you believe in self-love?
a) No, only those who are chronically unhappy and deeply troubled believe and need that shit.
b) Yes, in this time of hate, we all need to love ourselves more so we can love others more.
c) No, that's not allowed in Death Star, which I've sworn to protect.

6. Why are you so smart?
a) I'm not smart, only stupid people think they're smart
b) I've always worked hard and set the highest standards for myself. I took the most challenging courses and tasks and wouldn't accept anything less than an "A" at school and at work.
c) I'm naturally smart, it's God given.

7. How often do you screw up?
a) Rarely, and when I do, it's someone else's fault.
b) Never.
c) All the time, I'm such a fuck up..

8. Why are you so lazy?

a) I daydream a lot.
b) I'm not lazy.
c) I make excuses and blame others when something goes wrong..

9. Why are you so stupid?
a) I don't know what I don't know.
b) For the last time, I'm not stupid, I'm brilliant!
c) I've got to be if I'm filling this out..

10. What's Plato's Republic about?
a) **Why we're all dumbasses**
b) The meaning of life
c) How to be happy

11. How many hours a week does the CEO of Walmart work?
a) **100**
b) 70
c) 40

12. How many hours a week does Eminem work?
a) **100**
b) 70
c) 40
.

13. How many hours a week does 50 Cent work?
a) **100**
b) 70
c) 40

14. How many hours a week does Taylor Swift work?
a) **100**
b) 70
c) 40
.

15. What is Taylor Swift most likely doing right now?
a) Shaving off tied up Luke Skywalker's pubic hair with his light saber while singing Blank Space

b) Singing Teardrops on My Guitar while having sex with Anakin Skywalker as a tied up Padme watches
c) Doing take after take for her next video

16. What was Eminem likely doing on a random date, 2003?
a) Getting high and smacking his hoes
b) Working alone in a recording studio, repeating the same three lines over and over again because he demands perfection from himself.
c) Getting his dick licked by two of his dancers.
.

17. What does the CEO of Walmart do all day?
a) Figures out new ways to exploit hard workers like me.
b) Sets strategy and vision, negotiates partnerships, builds company culture, and manages supply chains to ensure consumers get what they want when they want it.
c) Pretending he's Jabba the Hut while banging his secretary dressed as Princess Leia
.

18. What was Tupac Shakur most likely doing during a typical evening?
a) Reading Machiavelli's The Prince.
b) Drinking his 40 and smacking his hoes like they're ewoks.
c) Having a threesome and some cocaine.

19. What was 50 Cent doing on a random Saturday night, 2006?
a) Getting fucked up his ass by his trainer, who resembles Han Solo
b) Working out, writing songs and negotiating business contracts.
c) Sucking your mom's big black dick, what the fuck does this have to do with the Dark Side?

20. Pick best sentence for first sentence of novel:
a) Dreary black skies loomed as the violent waves crashed onto glittering rocks that have never met such punishment.
b) It was a dark and stormy night; the rain fell in torrents —

except at occasional intervals, when it was checked by a violent gust of wind which swept up the streets.
c) Fucking hurricane knocking down trees.

21. Ten young women on a trip to a faraway land and stopped and robbed. Five are picked to be raped. What do you think the 5 NOT PICKED are thinking?
a) Whew, at least I wasn't raped!
b) I feel terrible for those who were raped.
c) Am I ugly?

22. How do you produce kids who will become batshit crazy as adults?
a) Tell them how wonderful and special they are, all the time.
b) Beat the shit out of them
c) Ignore them

23. Why are you so lazy?
a) I don't have many responsibilities
b) I'm not lazy, I give it my best every day.
c) It's too hard to think about the wants and needs of others.

24. What would you most likely pay money to watch?
a) Rabbit humping a growling cat
b) Tchaikovsky's Nutcracker Suite
c) Guy sucking his own dick.

25. What percentage of businesses fail within 5 years?
a) 50 percent
b) 20 percent
c) 2 percent

26. Are business owners entitled to a living wage?
a) Yes, everyone is entitled to a living wage.
b) No, it's business owner's fault she sucks at work and life
c) No, but we should set up programs to help business owners succeed.

27. Your partner tells you you're lazy. How do you respond?

a) Takes on to know one, asshole.
b) How am I lazy?
c) You never see all the things I do for you.

28. OPEN ENDED QUESTION
Person A from age 5 to 25, attends school 6 hours a day, studies 4 hours a day, spends 6 hours of leisure time learning to build and building, with like-minded friends, random things, like a tree house, a bridge, a dog walking robot. A also spends an hour per day daydreaming of building something that will improve the world's standard of living. At age 25, he graduates with a Masters degree in electrical engineering and is offered a salary of $150,000 to work as a product developer for a green tech company. He gets 3 weeks vacation, full benefits. He accepts the position and works 60-80 hours per week, and is expected to be available for phone calls and emails during his vacations. He pays the Federal Government 30 percent of his earnings.

Person B, from age 5-25, attends school 6 hours a day, studies 1 hour a day, spends 6 hours of leisure time passively watching TV shows and films like Jersey Shore and Twilight, 3 hours a day daydreaming about being wealthy and pampered and adored by everyone. At age 25, he graduates with a degree in Basic Bitch and a minor in Socks, Drugs, and Rock and Roll. Unable to find a job in his field of study, he takes a job as a cashier at McDonald's, making $12 per hour, 40 hours per week, or $24,000 a year. He doesn't have to pay taxes.

Let's assume one of them is "underpaid." Which one and why? (One sentence, keep it short).

Person A, because he's working on a product that might improve efficiency and reduce environmental damage.

29.. Pick best Golden Rule II
a) Treat others as you want to be treated.
b) Treat others as they want to be treated
c) Treat others as they treat others

Why are you so emotionally fragile?
a) My parents coddle and make excuses for me
b) I didn't have enough traumatic experiences during childhood.
c) I'm not fragile, I'm strong and brave! Smart and hard-working too!!!

31. Someone mugs you. Whose fault is it that you got mugged?
a) My fault
b) Society's
c) Mugger's

32. How many years SHOULD you spend in jail?
a) 0
b) 1-3
c) more than 3

33. OPEN ENDED QUESTION
Mary hires Peter and Paul to dig two ditches, assigning one to each. Peter finishes in one hour because he used his latest invention, the super-duper soil remover zapper. Paul, using a shovel, finishes his in 8 hours. How much should Mary pay Peter. How much to Paul? Whom should she hire if she wants a third ditch?

She should pay them the same and hire Peter to dig the third ditch.

34. How many hours did Peter spend developing his latest invention, the super-duper soil remover zapper?
a) 2, genius comes naturally to him
b) 200, he got a lucky break
c) 2000, innovation is hard work

35. Who is most likely to grow up batshit crazy?
a. Kid living in Syrian war zone
b. Middle-class White kid
c. Bill Gates's kids

36. The person who wrote this application:
a) Is an angry motherfucker.
b) Is batshit crazy. This is some fucked up shit.
c) Is trying to be funny. Ha ha. Ha. Right?

CHAPTER SIXTEEN -- SELECT APPLICATION QUESTIONS EXPLAINED

Pick best sentence:
a) Would you mind bringing me some beets when you get a chance?
b) Get beets now.
c) Hey fucktard, get your ass over there, get some beets and bring it over here.

Be concise. Most people are trained to say "A," as that's considered polite. It's actually stupid because more words means more communication errors and wasted time. Always choose to be more effective than polite.

Salesperson calls, asks "Hi, how are you doing today?" How do you respond?
a) What do you want?
b) I'm fine. How are you today?
c) I feel like shit. I want to beat the shit out of someone.

Translate what they're saying. "Hi, how are...today" = "Hi." Don't get involved in pointless small talk, don't waste time.

Pick best sentence for love-text:
a) Your scintillatingly luminous presence inspires and captiv-

ates my yearning heart to take an unsolicited leap of impossible faith into the great unknown of the comfort of your arms.
b) My darling, my heart aches for your presence and to finally be in your arms
c) Let's cuddle.

Be concise, avoid pretentiousness.

Your partner tells you you're lazy. How do you respond?
a) Takes one to know one, asshole.
b) Why am I lazy?
c) You never see all the things I do for you.

Always acknowledge what another person is feeling and thinking, even if you disagree. Unless you want a stupid fight that wastes time.

What happens when a school district gives middle-class high school students their own laptops?
a) Playing field is leveled, they perform almost as well as those rich privileged kids at elite private schools like Lakeside.
b) They use it to watch movies and play games, no change in academic performance.
c) They perform worse, laptops make people stupid. (Though a customer made a strong case for C).

All teenagers get this question right because they see first hand what's going on at school. Half their parents get this question right. Those who get it wrong are delusional. A couple of parents made a strong argument for "C," citing Silicon Valley CEOs who limit the time their teenagers use computers because computers hinder development of certain skills. But I don't think computers make people stupid. People make themselves stupid and they'll find a way to do that without computers.

Choosing A is dangerous. It's a stupid excuse that keeps people down.

Your 8 year old is new at school. He gets shoved out of the lunch line and is told to get to the back. He responds by beating the

shit out of the kid who bullied him. What's your response?
a) Ground him and make him apologize to the kid he beat up.
b) Tell him he did the right thing and to never worry about lawsuits, you'll take care of those if they come up.
c) Have your kid apologize to the kid he beat up and have them talk it out. End with a hug.

Something like this happened to a former employee and his parents told him he did right thing and to never worry about lawsuits. And this is what Eddie Huang (ABC sitcom Fresh Off the Boat is based on his life) did when he arrived at a new school. His father approved, from Huang's memoir, Fresh Off the Boat:

"A hardened, street-smart man, Louis had been sent by his own father to the United States to get him away from the hoodlums he had been running with in Taipei. "We wouldn't get in trouble with our dad if we got into a fight," Emery said. "We would get in trouble if we didn't win.""

Huang said the experience of earning people's respect made him who he is today. It made him feel that he controls his destiny.

Your daughter loves gymnastics and is about to enter her first meet. She's confident about winning and even thought about the perfect place to hang her blue ribbon. While she did well, she didn't medal, and was devastated. What do you, as a parent, tell her?
a) Tell her you thought she was the best
b) Tell her she has the ability and will surely win next time.
c) Tell her she doesn't deserve to win because she didn't work hard enough.

Lifted this question from a parenting site. Choice "A" is a lie (unless you're qualified to judge) and enough of these "nice and polite" lies will fuck someone up. Choice B can get you into more trouble, what happens if she doesn't win next time? And it doesn't address the reason why she didn't win, that she didn't work hard enough. Choice C teaches her that she's responsible for her place in society.

Someone leaves knives in soapy water. What do you do to make sure that person never does it again?
a) Tell her that doing that can hurt someone, that she needs to think about the consequences of her actions.
b) Lock her in the freezer for an hour.
c) Fill the sink with soapy water and knives. Have her wash knives.

You can't tell someone to be empathetic, you have to force them to experience what another person experiences. That's how you teach empathy.

How many hours a week does the CEO of Walmart work?
a) 100
b) 70
c) 30

Note: answer b is acceptable but not the best answer.

Purpose of the question is to see if applicant is capable of empathy (can you imagine what it's like to run Walmart); to gauge how likely applicant is to steal (how easily driven to envy); to get a sense of applicant work ethic and ability to think without bias (can you be fair to someone you don't like, and most applicants hate Walmart).

Those who answer 30 hours a week are, without exception, incapable of empathy, are crippled by envy, and hate any kind of work. They see the world as unfair, so why bother. We'll occasionally hire these people for part-time positions if they can do the job well enough. Those who write in their own answer "20" or "zero" are, without exception, batshit crazy and will spend most of their lives either in poverty or among the working poor. We won't go near them.

Someone who answers "100 hours a week" isn't necessarily capable of empathy...nor has a good work ethic. For instance, an upper-middle class kid with parents who work as executives at Amazon sees first-hand the 80 hour work weeks they put in. Unlike those who live in a world where 40 hours is a normal work week, he doesn't need to empathize to answer correctly. In another instance, a graduate of Northwestern University (an elite school) aced our application test. But his resume showed that he hadn't done much since graduating 6 years ago, he's a lazy piece of shit (and he knows it). But he answered the above question correctly because he was exposed, at Northwestern University, to the work ethic people are capable of having.

Those who have been exposed to the highest levels of competition are more likely to answer "100 hours" because they know what it takes to compete at such levels.

Owner teaches you to make something one way. Manager teaches you to do it another way. You're working with the manager, owner is watching. Whose way do you follow?
a) Manager's
b) Owner's
c) Do your own thing, show them you're a superstar!

When the manager is working, it's her space and staff are to follow her direction, even if the owner doesn't like what's happening. Manager's are given autonomy to do what they think is best. Owner will discuss it with the manager if he doesn't like her work.

Jane walks in and orders two 32 oz jars of juice, which will take you 15 minutes to make. Jared walks in immediately after she places her order and orders a small juice, which takes 2 minutes to make. Sam enters immediately after Jared places his order and orders a smoothie, which takes 30 seconds to make, whom do you serve first?
a) Jane
b) Jared
c) Sam

An empathy question. Jane expects a long wait. Having her wait 15 versus 20 minutes isn't going to matter, it won't feel any different to her. Neither Jared nor Sam expect to wait 20 minutes, they're expecting to be out within 5 minutes. Employees are expected to work with and manage customer expectations.

Cassie's daughter is throwing ice cubes at other customers. What do you do?
a) Tell them to "get the fuck out."
b) Politely ask Cassie to tell her daughter to stop
c) Throw ice cubes at them.

This happened at another restaurant. Manager chose "b" and customer responded with verbal altercation, creating an even bigger scene. Customer does this because most people choose "b" when she pulls this kind of shit, which she probably does all the time. Best to not begin discussion of what she's doing — she knows what she's doing and doesn't give a shit.

Option "C" would be fun — food fight! — but someone has to clean up.

You're the principal of the school. You visit a class where students are either goofing off or sleeping. What do you do?
a) Tell everyone that anyone who doesn't pay attention will get a failing grade for the day.
b) Don't do anything. Privately tell the teacher that he sucks at teaching, that's why nobody is listening.
c) Explain to students why it's important for them to pay attention to their teachers.

It's the teacher's job to make whatever he's teaching relevant to students. Students have a right to tune out if the teacher sucks. (I've taught before).

You're sampling drinks. What do you say to get someone to try one?

a) "Hi, would you like to try this?
b) "Try this."
c) "Drink this or I'll hit you."

Don't give people the option to reject your offer. Success rate is highest with "b."

Customer asks you what's the most popular drink. How do you respond?
a) Tell him what you think is most popular.
b) Ask him which flavors he prefers.
c) Ask the manager to answer his question.

Another empathy question. What is the customer really asking? He's having trouble deciding and is asking you to help him decide. He's asking "choose a drink I like." We train employees to respond to questions with a question.

As you're focused on a complicated order, condescending customer tells you that you should smile more if you want a tip. How do you respond?
a) "I'm sorry, I'm having a bad day."
b) Smile more.
c) Ask her if she'd like a side order of "Fuck Off" to go with her order…..

First, people have a right to feel whatever emotion they feel: to mourn when a loved one dies; to be angry when violated; to be happy when on cocaine. Second, focused people don't smile and focus is most important when doing something complicated. Third, we don't put up with customers this obnoxious.

How do you improve academic performance at a school?
a) Increase funding so facilities can be improved.
b) Increase number of (real) Asian students
c) Increase salaries so teachers perform better

Sense of reality question. Also gives us an opportunity to discuss touchy subjects with the applicant, to see how the applicant handles it.

Increasing salaries doesn't improve teacher performance, it only improves teacher retention and recruitment.

Quality of facilities doesn't correlate with student performance.

Increasing Asian enrollment (first and second generation only, and no jungle Asians like Filipinos unless they're ethnically Chinese), regardless of their socio-economic background, improves test scores of even the most ghetto schools (eg. Seward Park High School in the Lower East Side of NYC). How well students do is a matter of culture rather than finances.

Asian American students at a working class high school with crumbling facilities (Mark Keppel High School in California) score as well as Asian American counterparts at wealthy high schools with state of art facilities (San Marino High School in California).

PISA scores also show that there's little difference in test scores between wealthy and poor students in nations such as Vietnam and China, which may explain why there's so much upward and downward mobility in those nations. Only in nations that emphasize class differences, such as the US, do class differences affect test scores. (Probably because students internalize what they hear about themselves so stop giving poor kids an excuse to fail if you want them to succeed).

When you disaggregate US PISA scores by ethnicity, it shows that ethnic groups in the US score similarly as students from country of origin. Meaning, Mexican Americans score as well as Mexicans in Mexico; Taiwanese Americans score as well as Taiwanese students in Taiwan. Meaning, culture plays the most important role in educational outcomes.

CHAPTER SEVENTEEN -- OTHER APPLICATION QUESTIONS

We use these questions to get to know candidates better and to let them know about our work culture. Ultimately, we're more concerned about our ability to develop a candidate, regardless of his ability, knowledge, and attitude. The most difficult obstacle to overcome has been inflated self-esteem, which from our experience is correlated with low self-confidence.

We ignore applicants who think we ask these questions simply to be funny and thus respond with trite jokes. These are serious questions and we expect applicants to treat them as such.

July, Mount Baker. You arrive at a cabin. In the fridge there's a whole chicken (gizzards, feet, neck included), 5 eggs and 2 cups of flour. There's also a blender, a fork, a spatula, a pan, a water source, a crockpot, electricity, and a charcoal grill. You decide to make fried scrambled eggs. How do you make it and what else do you make?

Render fat from chicken to make scrambled eggs. Forage for whatever is in season, use wood for charcoal grill to make grilled chicken, make liver pate with blender, use gelatin from chicken feed, soup in a crockpot, the possibilities are endless. Point of this question is to test cooking skills, especially one's ability to cook without recipes. We also consider length of response – concise ones suggest no frills attitude, fast cook.

Do you run a trade deficit with a business? If you do, are you concerned about it?

Reading comprehension question, where we ask applicants to look up the definition of "trade deficit." Nearly all applicants haven't been able to comprehend trade deficits, usually confusing it with budget deficit. Seems that people often hear about trade deficits, usually as something problematic, but don't understand what it is. Anyway, nearly all of us carry a trade deficit with a business. For instance, I run a deficit with my grocers (I purchase more from them than they from me) and I'm not worried about it because they produce the goods I need to operate my business far more efficiently than I. Question tests applicant ability to understand and explain in plain language a simple concept. We suspect many didn't bother to look up the definition because they thought they already understand it.

Write your great-great granddaughter's obituary. Limit to 5 sentences.

In other words, tell us what the world looks like in the future i.e. its mores, technology, geopolitical boundaries. How old does she live till — 56, 207, 892? Where does she die – United States of Africa, planet Xenox in Alpha Centauri, Los Angeles the capital of Bermuda? How many spouses does she leave behind – one, four, any concubines? What does she die from, disease unknown to us, war with Klingons? Possibilities are endless. Main point is to use question to envision a different world. Question tests imagination and how an applicant understands self-being in relation to time and the world.

How did a grocery store cashier, making $9/hour, convince her employer to give her a $5/hour raise?

Cashier showed evidence that she generates, over the past year, double the sales per register than the average cashier and ranks first in accuracy. In other words, she's twice as fast as the average replacement and argued that her labor is therefore worth twice as much. Her boss, presented with QUANTIFIABLE evidence of her value, negotiated a $5/hour raise and promotion because he knew he'd save a lot of money by keeping her in place of hiring and training two replacement cashiers. Got nothing to do with how hard someone works (a useless subjective assessment) or how nice they are (most CEOs are not nice and I've asked my employees to not be nice). I don't care how "hard" my employees work. I only care that they bring value that exceeds the time and money I invest in them. Applicants who tell me that they're "hard workers" won't be hired because it's dangerous to hire anyone who thinks their pay should correlate to how hard THEY think they work (even if everyone else doesn't think he/she works hard). I never tell employees to work hard. I ask them to think of ways to increase their productivity. I ask them to work smart and responsibly. This question assesses how well one knows oneself and ability to understand a different frame of reference and to evaluate the value of one's work.

Why are you not special?

This question wards off those who think they're special.

Fight in the kitchen. Hot soup, butcher knife, last month's receipts. Which do you throw?

It's meant to be a fun question, a conversation starter. We ask how they made their choice.

Write the lyrics for the fictional song "When a Lamb Loves a Hungry Woman." Listen to "When a Man Loves a Woman" for rhythm and melody to match lyrics.

This question shows us an applicant's sense of humor and rhythm

PART III -- EMPLOYEES

I may be kindly, I am ordinarily gentle, but in my line of business I am obliged to will terribly what I will at all.
　-- Catherine the Great, empress of Russia

CHAPTER EIGHTEEN -- ON HUMAN NATURE

Summary: Manual for Alive Juice Bar managers.

I. Imitate the best. Treat employees and customers as they treat(ed) theirs.
a. Examples: Marco Pierre White; Charlie Trotter; Thomas Keller; David Chang

b. The best (from all fields) study and work with human nature. They're realists about themselves and other people.

II. Recognize human nature.
a. People don't change, even if they want to change. Personality is set by ~ age 6; habits by ~ 18; character by ~30. Growing wiser isn't the same as changing.

b. People can change temporarily. They revert back to their true (baseline) selves when overwhelmed or when they think they can get away with it.

c. People will deceive themselves and others to protect their identity.

d. People will rage against those who challenge their identity

e. Despite the self-deception, deep down people know who they really are, their proper place in society, and what's really going on within and around them.

III. Work with human nature
a. Don't try to change a person's sense of self. Never try to beat

self-deception. Let it be, work with it.

b. When trying to change behavior, focus on one or two at a time, and make it stick with repetition. Don't overwhelm someone by pointing out all mistakes. Change is painful work.

c. Telling and showing someone how to do something and watching them do it correctly once isn't enough. Mastery and change requires repetition. Drill the person — repetition — you're training. Create a habit so they don't have to think about what they're doing. Don't give someone the option to take short-cuts, to be lazy.

d. People revert back to their true state when overwhelmed by the difficulties of life. Prevent reversion by slowly increasing amount of stress one can handle. Tolerance for stress is a muscle that can grow stronger with training.

e. Once someone reverts back to their baseline state, they have to be retrained, just as with addicts.

f. People are more likely to do what you want them to do if they think it benefits them.

IV Manage Human Nature
a. People are contagious. We'll keep one emotionally disturbed knucklehead around. Any more and everyone gets infected.

b. People are contagious. Note the company an employee spends most time with. Wrong crowd means it's time to get rid of her.

c. People are contagious. Push employees to make progress in their lives, to strive for new achievements. It'll energize the crew and customers.

d. Mindset and attitude are more important than technical skills. People don't change, you can't change someone's mindset and attitude, you can't make someone coachable. But it's easy to teach someone who is coachable new technical skills.

That's why Charlie Trotter hired those without restaurant experience.

e. Trust your guts, never your heart. Your gut is the subconscious processing reality, often into uncomfortable truths about yourself and others. Your heart tells you what you want to hear, which is rarely the truth.

f. Use fear to manage employees and customers. If there's no fear, there's no respect. If there's no respect, there's no love.

CHAPTER NINETEEN -- HOW TO SPOT BULLSHIT

I. Bullshit is Everywhere
From Time magazine, 2014:

Chinese troops violently retook the square in Beijing where pro-democracy protesters had set up camp for weeks. The Tiananmen Square massacre left an unknown number dead, with some estimates in the thousands, and smothered a democratic movement. But after a quarter-century—and a thorough attempt by the Chinese government to conceal the events that unfolded that June—our collective memory is sometimes limited to not much more than an image of a man defiantly standing in front of a tank.

Imagine the massacre, what it looked like.

Now watch the "tank man" video on youtube. Search for "tank man." No, do it now, motherfucker.

Watch the entire fucking thing you lazy piece of shit, especially if you were born before 1980. I'll make this worth the two and a half minutes of your time, this will blow your mind.

What did you see? Pick:

a. Brave Chinaman standing up for democracy and human rights
b. Lunatic Chinaman doing some crazy shit.

Now what did the tank do? What the fuck did the tank do?

a. Crushed the Chinaman.
b. Tried to go around the Chinaman.

Is your bullshit detector on? What did you see? What did you read? Does everything make sense or do you sense dissonance between what you saw and what you read?

I saw a battalion of tanks show remarkable restraint. Tank didn't even react when the Chinaman climbed on top of it. Now stand on the top of a police car in the US and see what happens to you.

Now read this, from Wikileaks:

"He watched the military enter the square and did not observe any mass firing of weapons into the crowds, although sporadic gunfire was heard. He said that most of the troops which entered the square were actually armed only with anti-riot gear – truncheons and wooden clubs; they were backed up by armed soldiers," a cable from July 1989 said.

And then this, from former Australian diplomat Gregory Clark writing in Japan Times:

Over the years the "black information" people in the U.S. and U.K. governments have had some spectacular successes...But the greatest achievement of them all still has to be the myth of a June 4, 1989, Tiananmen Square massacre, with talk of hundreds if not thousands of protesting students mowed down by military machine guns.

What really happened? More from Clark:

In recent years the Tiananmen massacre story has taken something of a beating as people in the square that night, including a Spanish TV unit, have emerged to tell us that there was no massacre, that the only thing they saw was a military unit entering in the late evening and asking the several hundred students still there quietly to leave

So who is full of shit, the Chinese government or Time magazine? Time piece of shit magazine, that's who and this isn't the only bullshit that gets tossed at us. Now ask yourself why nearly all Americans who followed news of this incident believed it even when there isn't one video or photo showing systematic killing of students in the Square? (There are only videos of riots in parts of the city, which all parties agree happened). What makes people susceptible to believing bullshit?

Good managers can spot bullshit. And there's a lot of bullshit out there — most of it is bullshit — people's delusions about themselves and others count as bullshit too. Spot bullshit by relying more on a person's actions and the results of their actions, less on what a person says. Words are meaningless until backed by action and results.

II. Why People are Full of Shit

You can learn a lot about a person by noting what type of bullshit he believes in. A few years back there was a report on the news about a pitbulls killing a boxer at a Seattle dog park. Description of pitbulls' owners, from Mountlake Terrace News:

The couple is described as a heavily tattoo (sic) man in his 20's and a female 5'6 190 lbs late in her 20's with three pit bulls.

(Identified as White in another description).

In other words, whiggers. Yes yes, it makes sense, so much sense…

Except it didn't to those who paid attention to the improbability of some of the details of the report. Which you're not likely to do if you secretly hate whiggers (which is a more socially acceptable way of expressing hatred of Black people). At any rate, it turned out to be a hoax, a bullshit report that led to hysteria and two weeks worth of copycat bullshit reports of pitbulls throughout the Puget Sound region mauling this dog and that dog while their whigger owners stood there laughing.

Point is, people will believe that which confirms their reality. And not believe that which challenges their identity. That's why there's so much bullshit, why people lie to themselves and to others, with those from Anglo cultures doing it the most.

Good managers are adept at recognizing and managing employee and customer realities and identities. The self-described "nice girl" will find it difficult to recognize her inconsiderate behavior and if she does, will excuse it or blame others. The guy who thinks he's funny won't notice that nobody is laughing at his jokes. The customer who thinks he's being polite when he doesn't tell the employee that there's something wrong with a product won't realize that he's a cowardly narcissist who is hurting the business by not letting anyone know.

III. How to Detect Bullshit

Train yourself to spot signs of bullshit and how to translate what someone is really saying by focusing on their actions.

Deflection instead of taking responsibility. If you point out to an employee that he did something wrong and he responds with: "Oh I usually do it right I just messed up that one time," he's full of shit and will make that same mistake again, guaranteed.

Anyone who is wordy is full of shit. They're like students answering short essay questions. The ones who know the answer get to the point and give the correct answer with precision and alacrity. Those who don't know guess this and that in hopes of getting partial credit. Never trust someone who rambles, who can't stick to a topic.

Anyone who uses a lot of jargon is full of shit. Jargon is meant to intimidate and confuse so you don't call them out on their bullshit.

Those who name-drop are full of shit. Also used to intimidate.

Changing the topic means there's bullshit and the problem will not be solved.

Blaming others and making excuses means there's bullshit. This one happens all the time.

Gift giving can be a sign of bullshit to come or to cover/make up for. Dad buys his daughter a new car because he feels guilty about divorcing her mom. Girl gives a super nice but too nice boyfriend a really good blowjob before breaking up with him the next day. Giving a compliment to fish for a compliment. Dude telling his wife he loves her after losing a month's worth of salary at the casino.

Those who fish for compliments, who are addicted to praise and affirmation, are full of shit and have no integrity. You can't have principles when you're addicted to praise because you'll change your story, you'll do whatever it takes -- lying usually -- to make someone like and praise you.

Examples:

"Happy Birthday, Love you Dad!"
Translation: "I love you because I seek your affirmation that I'm a good daughter. But I don't love you enough to plan how I'm going to take care of you when you turn geriatric. Your affirmation isn't worth that much trouble."

Note: Love is an action, not a feeling. Love is communicated through words when there's little or no action. (Which is why Americans say "love" so much).

"Honey, I got your dry cleaning!"
Translation: "Take me to this show and dinner and then play with my pussy for a long time when we get home. I earned it."

Note: Fishing for acknowledgement is one of the lowest forms of emotional manipulation. It suggests score keeping, which is impossible to maintain if one wants a healthy relationship.

CHAPTER TWENTY -- TRAINING NEW EMPLOYEE GUIDELINES

Here's how we train new employees.

Attitude and Demeanor
Several will train new hires. Attitude, demeanor, and approach to training must be consistent across all trainers. Lack of consistency will make new hires confused and wondering if there are double standards. Highest ranking trainer sets the tone and approach, which can be adjusted based on circumstances. Tone and approach must always be customized based on personality and skill level of new hire.

Don't try to be friends with new hires during their training period. Most hires don't make it through this period and you need to be an objective evaluator.

Observe
Good trainers don't simply tell trainees what to do. They observe trainees at all times. Be sure they're operating with all of their senses. It's especially important to look at what their eyes are looking at, as it'll show you their court vision, how much they're able to see. Those who look down are out of it, looking inward, and are only able to handle one task at a time. Those who are looking up are searching for something in the exter-

nal world and are capable of handling multiple customers while running multiple processes.

Listen to the rhythm of their work, you can hear the sound of bad cooking. If the sound of something is off, if you hear hesitation or choppiness, correct it before it becomes a habit.

Observe their character. Look for all of the seven deadly sins: sloth, greed, wrath, vanity, gluttony, lust, and envy. If there's envy and/or greed, there's going to be theft. If there's vanity (narcissism), there's going to be bad customer service, where the employee only talks about herself instead of focusing on the wants and needs of the customer.

Method

Give them an hour to get comfortable, then scare the shit out of them to see how comfortable they are with being uncomfortable. We're testing for mental toughness and the ability to function under pressure. If they can't handle difficult situations with grace and aplomb, they're out. The world doesn't conform to anyone. It's the individual's job to adapt to evolving circumstances and contexts.

Ask trainees challenging questions. For instance, what's the final ingredient that goes in the veggie juice if the next drink is a green energizer? Make them figure out solutions to problems on their own instead of telling them how to do something. Ask them to identify problems. You'll learn a lot about them quickly. Unless it's busy, avoid telling them what to do.

Help trainees simplify what they see so they can learn the menu quickly. There are only a few drink items that need to be memorized. The remaining items are variations of those. For instance, Exercist is Veggie Juice plus Apple, or Sweet Version of Veggie Juice. Help them recognize patterns throughout the store and menu.

Drill them on basic nutritional information (eg how many calories in 2 tbls of peanut butter).

Teach them to trust their instincts and intuition, train them to not follow recipes (we don't use any).. Don't let them read the menu when making drinks. There are only a few processes and facts they need to memorize. The rest they should be able to figure out. Have them talk, think their way to the correct formula. If it's busy, tell them what to put in the drink. If you're slammed, make it yourself.

Play-act scenarios. Prepare them for the unexpected. Use this to break habits, to test their knowledge, and to assess how they handle unusual requests. A common one we practice is when a customer asks what's popular or what your favorite is. The correct response is to ask questions about their preferences.

CHAPTER TWENTY ONE -- PASSAGE OF SEATTLE'S $15HOUR MINIMUM WAGE: NOTES AND PREDICTIONS

Note: this was written in 2015, the year Seattle's $15 minimum wage law was passed.

Doom and gloom for Seattle?
No. $15/hour will, ironically, accelerate gentrification in Seattle. Spatial divide between socio-economic classes will become even more pronounced, with the middle-class moving to first ring suburbs, the poor to outer ring suburbs (as has been the trend). Seattle becomes city of champagne socialists ("privileged" lefties) and the homeless. Kinda like San Fran.

There will be fewer McDonald's, Jack n' Boxes, Olive Gardens, anything considered to attract the "poor," the "deplorables," anyone who disgusts champagne socialists. "Dirty" industries that employ low-skilled labor move to suburbs (or another state), allowing developers to — after years of resistance from Labor — transform SoDo into mixed use high end neighborhood. (While champagne socialists become so because of guilt over their privileged upbringing, they remain so not out of conviction or care for those less privileged, but because their political and social philosophy works for them economically and socially. They get what they want, and look good doing so).

This is like Rent Control in NYC and SF (version of which may be legislated in Seattle). Government intervenes to ensure socioeconomic diversity, to maintain cultural vibrancy of whatever whatever I call bullshit. End result will be more spatial and social segregation, not less. (Anthony Bourdain paints similar picture in his graphic novel "Get Jiro!").

Molly Moon Ice Cream supports 15 min because it would increase consumer spending. Agree?
Not sure. To begin with, how will they spend? On high or low return on investment activities and items? Random novelties, twinkies, meth, and mindless escapes that shrink the economic pie? Or a CPA textbook, math tutor, energizing food, challenging activities that grow the pie? My guess is those who are chronically making minimum wage are those who waste most of their leisure time on activities that produce little to negative value (getting wasted and causing 10 car accident is example of negative value act). Giving such workers higher pay will shrink the economy. I'm also guessing that these workers will be laid off and will find more appropriate jobs in, say, Everett, where pay will reflect the value of their work. Those who produce $10/hour worth of work don't get $15/hour. Not even in the most fantastic Leninist state.

I suspect businesses supporting 15 minimum are referencing Henry Ford's controversial "$5 a day minimum" at his factories. Short version: Ford increased minimum wage at his factories from $2.34 for 9 hours to $5.00 for 8. Business leaders howled, claimed that the money would be wasted on vices. Result: Ford was sorta right. Productivity soared and a new middle-class emerged with enough money to purchase the products (autos) they made.

I say "sorta" because Ford didn't offer his wages to anyone. He hired social workers to investigate the habits of potential and existing employees. So more likely, the higher wage didn't make employees more productive. Ford improved productivity because of the thoroughness of his background checks and his wages attracted and retained the best applicants.

Whereas I'm hearing something different from 15 NOW supporters, a contrasting interpretation of history. That raising the wage of a worker will make her more productive *and* transform her into someone champagne socialists won't hold in maternal contempt. But that's not what happened in Ford's case. Ford simply did a better job at finding and attracting underpaid employees.

Sure sure, there are underpaid employees under the current wage regime. These workers probably will save and invest more, and perhaps spend more at high value businesses. Not because they earn more, but because they've always had the desire to do so. Increasing wages doesn't change a person. It only changes their actions, shows us who they really are.

The person who has been working as a cook at Jack N Box isn't going to eat at Harvest Vine or the Corson Building even if you pay him a six figure salary. He's going to eat at McDonald's for lunch, Buca Di Beppo for his birthday, not because he's poor, but because THAT'S WHAT HE LIKES AND WANTS. If he really wants to eat at Cafe Juanita, he would, he'd figure out a way to make it happen, either by working there or someplace similar. The kid making $12 an hour who eats at Thrive does so not because he's rich — he's not — but because THAT'S WHAT HE LIKES AND WANTS, and so he makes it happen.

What happens when a chronic minimum wage worker wins the lottery? They lose it all, fuck up in their own fucked up way: spend on bling and bad investments and attract the worst type of people. More money didn't transform them, it only brought attention to their character.

Thomas Jefferson understood that wealth and dignity must be accumulated slowly, through hard work and thrift. That's why he envisioned the USA as an agrarian rather than an urban industrial nation. He understood that wealth accumulated too quickly brings out the worst in people — ask former NBA player Jalen Rose about how many young NBA players squander their wealth. One appreciates wealth only after earning it slowly, over a life-time.

Will higher wages mean less dependence on government agencies?
No. Once established, government agencies are notoriously difficult to close. Someone will figure out a way to make $15/hour the new poverty wage. Poverty is a psychological condition that's based on comparisons of material wealth — envy — rather than a physiological situation. Few in the United States are starving to death. Many don't want to be known as someone who makes minimum wage, regardless of what that wage is.

15 Minimum wage will lift many out of poverty.
It will not. Poverty is a mindset, an attitude, not an economic condition. Money doesn't make one dignified. Dignity comes with conviction, resilience, and grit. Those who lack dignity at 10 dollars an hour will lack it at 15 dollars an hour, at 50 an hour, 500, it doesn't matter. That's why so many big pot lottery winners lose everything in a few years.

Will the new minimum wage affect Alive Juice Bar?
Probably not much. There's enough time for distributors to relocate so we don't expect dramatic price increases.

Would you open a store in Seattle?
Fuck no!

CHAPTER TWENTY TWO -- THE $15/HOUR MINIMUM WAGE: BRING IT ON, MOTHERFUCKERS.

Restaurant owners are freaking out about surviving a $15 minimum wage. I hope the $15/hour minimum wage proposal IS passed into law, even though I don't think the government should be involved in a labor contract between two private parties. I'm just curious about what would happen to Puget Sound region restaurants, the culinary landscape and socio-cultural life.

"You sick fuck," some of you are thinking. "That's like saying you want to be gang banged until your asshole looks like a donut just to see if you'd enjoy it."

Sure, if you say so. I really don't think it'll be that bad. A few reasons why:

1. Shit like this has happened before. Like back in 1988, I-518 increased the wage of tipped workers by 85%. Yet the restaurant scene is as strong as ever. And we still have Dick's, Teriyaki, McDonald's, Olive Garden.

2. Free agency didn't destroy baseball, as some predicted. At-

tendance has risen and big market teams are LESS dominant than they were in the pre-free agency era. And baseball players get paid 10 times more than they would without free agency.

3. Shortly after her arrival to New York City and prior to recording her first single, Madonna was raped at knifepoint. She didn't report it. What does this have to do with the price of kale?

4. Koreatown, Los Angeles. Destroyed in 1992 LA Riots. Today, it's thriving, the most cosmopolitan and dense LA neighborhood, and the center of LA nightlife.

5. Banning smoking in taverns didn't put most of them out of business.

6. It's 1910. You own stagecoaches. Some dickhead named Ford starts mass producing automobiles. Your business is falling apart as people increasingly opt for autos to get around. Should anyone care?

7. You own a turnkey restaurant that makes you a solid income. Some family opens a similar restaurant a couple blocks away. Entire family works in the restaurant, no employees. Since they live 6 in a three bedroom, 1200 sq house in a modest neighborhood, they're able to undercut you on price. Forcing you out of business. Should anyone care?

Point is, it doesn't matter what happens. Shit happens. It's the business owner's responsibility to figure out how to make it work, to cooperate with an unpredictable world. So let's think about contingency plans. Business owners don't deserve a certain lifestyle any more than do minimum wage workers.

Thought project. What happens at $15/hour to following businesses?

Busy McDonald's Franchise: Estimate $15,000 worth of increased labor costs per month, assuming staff of six (manager and assistant manager not included), 20 hours per day. That's $180,000 per year. That won't work for most franchisees. Solution, replace two employees with self-serve registers, like the ones we see in unionized grocery stores. One employee — likely assistant manager — handles three registers. The technology is already there, they're just waiting for the moment labor costs exceed technology costs. Robot making burgers are also available (expensive) if the owner wants to further reduce staff.

Moderately busy Subway Franchise: Having trouble seeing which processes they can automate. There would need to be a major overhaul of current processes for automation to happen. To maintain profitability, Subway franchise would have to be family owned and operated (as is increasingly the case, with South Asian immigrant families taking the lead), with perhaps one 30 hour a week, high value employee (assistant manager). In this scenario, increased labor cost is insignificant. It'd be like dealing with gas prices tripling within a year. Those who treat franchises as turn-key operations won't make it (as is often the case anyway).

Highly regarded bistros and fine dining establishments. They'll professionalize service jobs. Tips will be included in the bill, servers and bartenders will be paid a wage plus benefits, including sick time and paid vacation. That's what Herbfarm does. That's how it's done in France. Professionalization further reduces turnover and improves service.

Low-End chain restaurants like Olive Garden. I don't know how they survive now. And because of their low status and difficult customers, they'll have a difficult time attracting professional service workers. But they seem to figure it out.

Alive Juice Bar. Similar to Subway, it will need to be family owned and operated (grandma grandpa, teenager kids, mom and dad, similar to how Pho and Teriyaki restaurants are operated) to remain profitable. One option is to reduce hours to 6am-3pm and work alone. Would make the same amount as I do now AND work less (managing, training, and hiring takes a lot of time). In fact, I'd look forward to not subjecting my date to interruptions during dinner. Professionalization of positions — increasing prices — isn't an option because we're take-out fast-food. Customers aren't obligated to tip. Another option is to reduce staff and work longer hours. Would make significantly more than before. Will also look into technology that allows customers to place and pay for order from their phone. Continue to encourage paying with a credit card to check themselves out.

The point is that there's always a way to survive. I'm predicting that $15/hour will, long-term, spur new technological innovations that will at least double worker productivity (increased pay does NOT improve productivity. Technological advances and lower turnover do. The incompetent will remain so regardless of pay). Meaning, real labor costs will go down, and businesses will be more profitable than ever. How else can we explain the increased productivity and fairly stable unemployment rate after every minimum wage increase?

(The person watching over 4 grocery self-checkout stands is more productive not because he's exerting more energy, but because the technology allows him to do the work of 2-3 employees working a traditional check out line. Don't ever think higher pay spurs one to work harder. It does not. No evidence. But plenty of counter-evidence).

As for those laid off, technological innovation will make them employable again, as has always been the case. For instance, timed-cooking technology used at McDonald's and Appleby's allowed those who can't figure out with their senses when a burger is done or a steak is medium rare to be productive enough to work the line. Advanced cash registers allow those who can't do arithmetic to be productive. Spell-check may allow an administrative assistant who struggles with spelling to keep his job.

The only concern is that by dumbing down jobs — as Starbucks has over the past two decades to support their expansion — we're creating an unskilled workforce that will never become skilled, never enjoy creative work. More troubling, they will become even more culturally and socially estranged from those creating the technology necessary to keep businesses running and people employed and productive. Will continued resentment and envy be inevitable? Will $15/hour become the new poverty wage?\

CHAPTER TWENTY THREE -- WHAT'S A FAIR WAGE?

Someone mentioned that we're obligated to pay Fast Food workers a so-called "living wage" because they work dead end jobs. Bullshit. former McDonald's CEO Charlie Bell started working at McDonald's at age 15. At 19, he was the youngest store manager ever in Australia. Managing director at 29, CEO at 42. Not bad for someone without a college degree. Say what you want about McDonald's menu, but they provide far better career opportunities than do small businesses like Alive Juice Bar. One has a much better chance of making a million bucks a year working for McDonald's than at Alive Juice Bar. Or at Tom Douglas Restaurants. Or as a corporate lawyer at Skadden Arps. Or as a surgeon at UW Hospitals. I don't see the dead-end. I only hear people wrongly assume that because there are a lot of people who never end up making "living wage" at Fast Food restaurants means they're in dead-end jobs.

"But these people who aren't management material still need a so-called living wage," some argue. "It's not their fault they don't have the ability to work their way up to a living wage."

So stick the bill to the employer. Blame the business, even though the source of the dead-end mentality that prevents a Fast Food worker from ever rising to management is more likely found at home and in schools. So stick the entire bill to the business even though we're collectively at fault for producing masses of spiritless and aimless citizens and workers? To those who want to raise the minimum wage to $15/hour, who rail against the injustice of the current minimum wage, how about YOU do the right thing and hire minimum wage workers to work for YOU at $15/hour. The additional competition for their labor will force Fast Food businesses to raise wages, right? Have them walk your dog, clean your house, wipe your ass, mow your lawn, discipline your kids, feed your cats, suck your dick, whatever, I'm sure you can figure out how to use someone to make you more productive and your life a bit easier. And be sure to give them at least four hour shifts.

A McDonald's manager without a (useless) college degree makes $42000 a year. A staff accountant fresh out of college makes the same. Let's say it took McDonald's manager three years to reach his position, during which he made $10-$13 dollars an hour and was sent to Hamburger U (this is real school, not trying to be funny) to take business management classes, free of charge. Took accountant four years of college to obtain the degree necessary to attain her position. Accountant has to pay for her degree. The accountant also works 500 more hours a year than does the McDonald's manager.

Who's better off, the kid who got a job at McDonald's after high school and worked his way up to management or the accountant who went to college after high school and is now 50k in debt? I don't see how an entry level job at McDonald's is a dead end.

What about surgeons? Four years undergrad taking an extremely difficult courseload; a year to prepare for MCATs; four years in medical school, where professors routinely call you a "nitwit" and "dumb fuck." Then five to six years as an intern, making $60,000 a year while working 100 hours a week and your boss routinely calls you a "moron." You're $400,000 in debt so $60,000 is actually closer to $25,000 a year. One hundred hours a week at $25,000 a year is BELOW minimum wage.

Sure sure, so the vascular surgeon will make $400,000 a year 10 years after finishing residency. But Charlie Bell, who didn't go to college, was making more than that when he was 29 years old working for McDonald's!

There aren't many jobs that pay well at first (engineering is an exception). Sure sure, the financial analyst fresh out of college makes 80k a year. She also works 100 hours a week. Her hourly wage is comparable to that of a security guard. The McDonald's manager likely makes more per hour.

The question then: if Fast Food workers need more money to live, why don't they get second or third jobs? (Some do, usually immigrants). Eighty hours a week at $10 an hour, that's 40k a year. That's sufficient, twice as much as grad student TAs and RAs make. And as pointed out before, there's room to grow for those who work on their leadership and management skills. Those who don't develop adequate management skills, read Part I again.

In a free market (no cartels, no unions), people are paid based on value they produce for a business. How much one is paid has nothing to do with how gross a job is, or how "hard" someone works. Produce value that exceeds money paid to you and you keep your job. Produce value that exceeds many times over money paid to you and you'll be promoted and given a raise. Produce negative value — your fuck ups cost money to fix — and you're fired. It's that simple, yet nearly all my applicants don't know how to calculate the value of their labor. It's why so many of them are slowly killing themselves with envy.

CHAPTER TWENTY FOUR -- WHAT'S A LIVING WAGE?

So what's a "living wage?" How much space does one need to live "comfortably?" In New York City, a 300 sf studio apartment inhabited by one person is considered by some as luxurious. In Seattle, most would consider such a space as cramped. Avant-garde architects have been designing 150 sf houses, offering them as appropriate for most people.

How much and what type of food does one need to eat well? Should shopping at Whole Foods be a "human right?" Two hundred bucks a week for a family of four? Or would four dollars per week be enough?

Now imagine a world where everyone you consider poor no longer exists. Would that be the end of poverty? Or would those you consider middle-class become the new poor? Now ask yourself if you prefer to be Charlemagne, who ruled France from 768 to 816 or something, or would it be better to live in the present, in the Puget Sound region, making $30,000 a year as a McDonald's cook, no children, basically living what many would consider a lower middle-class social and economic life? Would you prefer to be king in a world without plumbing, electricity, autos, planes, modern medical care, or the internet, or would it be better to be almost "poor" in present day Seattle?

That poverty is a relative concept and "poor people" is a social construct aren't new ideas. In fact, it's obvious. But too often, how we analyze and interpret the world is framed by academic readings of government created constructs such as race, gender, economic class. I'm not arguing that these constructs are useless. Nor am I saying that these constructs necessarily foment racism, sexism, class warfare, nationalism, and so forth. They're, when used appropriately, very helpful — think about why your doctor asks you to categorize yourself in terms of race, age, gender, etc. But these constructs can also make it tempting to confuse cause and effect and difficult to find patterns of behavior that traverse social identity and place. It can spawn asinine public policy concepts such as "living wage" that promote a sense of helplessness among those who identify as or feel poor.

Being "poor" or living in "poverty" is an attitude, a mindset, not an economic condition. It has nothing to do with how much money one has. Someone with a poverty mindset may only be able to get a candy bar out of a dollar. Another person may be able to make a feast of stone soup, enough to feed 10, out of the same amount. There's no limit to what the human mind can create. The possibilities are endless. There's no such thing as a "living wage." We don't know what someone can do with a square foot of living space. We don't know how many meals someone can make out of a dollar. By insisting there's such a thing as a "living wage" and a "poverty line," we give a lot of people an excuse to be envious, miserable, wasteful, and passive instead of grateful, optimistic, frugal, and creative.

Point is, "living wage" is a ridiculous concept. I'm ok with socially constructed categories, some of them are useful. Like race, class, and gender, however unstable and problematic they may be. "Living wage" only serves the interest of the government and gives many yet another reason to beg for life. It frames and limits what's possible in life. It crushes the spirit and will to live of those who don't make a "living wage." And nearly every business owner I've met has spent a few years not making a "living wage," some not able to feed their young children "properly."

Do business owners deserve a "living wage"? Absolutely not.

CHAPTER TWENTY FIVE -- WHO DESERVES A "LIVING WAGE"?

Should there be a law requiring business owners to pay themselves a "living wage." And if a business owner can't afford to pay herself such a wage, then should the government intervene to insure the owner is paid a living wage? I suspect most conservatives and liberals are in agreement about this law -- it's ridiculous, ethically and practically. Few are willing to pay for someone's fuck ups. Tornado or a pandemic destroys a business, fine, let's consider a bailout. But a bailout for incompetence?

Ridiculous, says the liberal, because it's the business owner's fault when her business fails. She didn't work hard enough, she didn't treat employees and customers well, she had a bad idea. In other words — and this is a tough one to get the left to admit — a so-called "living wage" isn't an American, much less universal, right, a living wage has to be earned. It's HER fault and taxpayers shouldn't have to pay for HER fuck ups.

Fair enough and I think most conservatives would agree. But shouldn't this line of reasoning be applied to everyone, including those making minimum wage? If a business fails because its owner is lazy or a dumbass — and most businesses fail within two years, sometimes leaving its owners destitute and homeless — then what should we say about the person who can't seem to get beyond minimum wage and rise to management position? Left says such workers are exploited. Right calls them lazy. Which is it?

Here's a question I ask applicants:

Who is overpaid?
a) Microsoft Engineer making $150,000 a year, full benefits, 3 weeks paid vacation, matching 401k.
b) McDonald's Cook making $10/hour, no benefits, no paid vacation.
c) Police Officer making $80,000 a year, full benefits, 4 weeks paid vacation, lifetime pension after retirement (20 years service).

Nearly all applicants pick "A."

Later, I ask the same question in a different form:

Person A from age 5 to 25, attends school 6 hours a day, studies 4 hours a day, spends 6 hours of leisure time learning to build and building, with like-minded friends, random things, like a tree house, a bridge, a dog walking robot. A also spends an hour per day daydreaming of building something that will improve the world's standard of living. At age 25, he graduates with a Masters degree in electrical engineering and is offered a salary of $150,000 to work as a product developer for a green tech company. He gets 3 weeks vacation, full benefits. He accepts the position and works 60-80 hours per week, and is expected to be available for phone calls and emails during his vacations. He pays the Federal Government 30 percent of his earnings.

Person B, from age 5-25, attends school 6 hours a day, studies 1 hour a day, spends 6 hours of leisure time passively watching TV shows and films like Jersey Shore and Twilight, 3 hours a day daydreaming about being wealthy and pampered and adored by everyone. At age 25, he graduates with a degree in Socks, Drugs, and Rock and Roll. Unable to find a job in his field of study, he takes a job as a cashier at McDonald's, making $10 per hour, 40 hours per week, or $20,000

for the year. He doesn't have to pay taxes.
Let's assume one of them is "underpaid." Which one and why?

Nearly all applicants pick Person A. Meaning nearly all of my applicants are confused -- they want justice and equality of outcomes, which isn't possible because everyone is different.

So, which is it? Is the minimum wage worker underpaid or not? Is he getting what he deserves? Summary of this chapter in three questions:

a) Is a living wage a universal right?
b) Should all business owners be paid a "living wage" and be protected by labor laws?
c) Do all employees deserve a "living wage"?

CHAPTER TWENTY SIX -- JOBS FOR ALL = DUMBFUCKINGEST IDEA EVER

Dumber than the second dumbest idea — "free college for all" — because I can at least imagine that program helping a few people (and hurting most) while jobs for all fucks everything up for everyone.

To begin with, most people are unemployable *in the present economy*. Just because someone has a job doesn't mean that that person is employable — "suitable for paid work" — most who work are just live bodies filling in space that needs to be filled, like the kid stuck in right field because he can't catch a pillow thrown at him. And then there are those who are unemployable because they consistently produce negative value: give them a dish to wash and they'll break it; a car to transport things and they'll run over people; a bank to run and they'll start a nation-wide recession. There are plenty of those and the goal should be to keep most people from working, not to give people jobs they're sure to fuck up.

The Pareto Principle: the 80/20 Rule
Once upon a time, an Italian renaissance man named Vilfredo Pareto noticed that ~80 percent of the peas in his garden came from ~20 percent of the pods. He looked around some more and

saw that ~80 percent of land in Italy was owned by ~20 percent of Italian citizens. And 80 percent of the food was grown on 20 percent of agricultural land. This 80/20 is everywhere.

For instance, 80 percent of wealth is owned by 20 percent of the population, and that's typically true across all nations (aberrations are eventually self-corrected). Eighty percent of Microsoft Word users use 20 percent of its features, while 20 percent of users use 80 percent of its features. Twenty percent of employees generate 80 percent of revenue and vice versa. Twenty percent of people commit 80 percent of crimes and vice versa. You get the idea, the Pareto Principle is a law of nature and when you go against the law, you get something like the Killing Fields —disaster.

Pol Pot was a Social Justice Warrior. He executed 1.5 million of his countrypeople in the name of social justice.

It's always been this way, most people have been un or barely employable, regardless of era and regime, and that's never going to change. Men sitting in basements jerking off and playing video games isn't a unique symptom of our post-industrial society, it's a variation of what men have been doing for centuries, except ours is less violent because the routine acts of violence are virtual rather than real thanks to Nintendo and Playstation.

Examples

Customer who is a Boeing engineer told me that she mostly goofs off at work (and she was concerned about what that was doing to her work ethic and mental health). The reason she goofs off is because her manager isn't an engineer, he has an MBA and has no idea how long it should take an engineer to solve an engineering problem. He gives her, for instance, two weeks to complete an assignment she finishes in four hours.

So who hired the barely competent, hardly qualified project manager who is too lazy to ask his staff how long it takes them to finish a task? Incompetent human resources executives who hire incompetent human resource administrators who hire people based on degrees of questionable value (e.g. MBA) instead of their competencies. Beginning to see how 80 percent of employees in a business can contribute so little to a project yet keep their jobs, including executive ones? An aside: you can't study business the way you can Math, Physics and Logic. Running a business is more of an art than a science — the context (e.g. regulations, taxes, weather, culture) is constantly changing and no two businesses are alike. It's not like Math, where 2+2=4 no matter the weather, the tax laws, and who is president of the United States. In Math and Physics, a consensus is possible. In business, it isn't and when someone insists it is, it leads to disaster, like nosediving demon planes. Now let's get back to the question about the prevalence of incompetence in the workplace. From the New Republic's investigative news article Crash Course: How Boeing's Managerial Revolution led to the 737 Max Disaster, "the

Boeing assembly line that opened in 2011 had for years churned out scores of whistle-blower complaints and wrongful termination law-

suits packed with scenes wherein quality-control documents were regularly forged, employees who enforced standards were sabotaged, and planes were routinely delivered to airlines with loose screws, scratched windows, and random debris everywhere.

Oops, Boeing 737 goes splat!

How about high school counselors, how many of them are good at advising students on coursework, college and career options, and life in general? Or do most regurgitate basic basic info that's easily found online? Here's a test you can give to a high school counselor, see how many can answer these questions off the top of their heads:

Identify the following schools, which state each is located and what each is known for:

a) Williams College
b) Bryn Mawr College
c) CalTech University
d) Harvey Mudd College

What percentage of counselors have an informed opinion about any of the schools listed? Now these aren't some fringe schools that don't matter, these are some of the most prestigious schools in the US that every competent high school counselor needs to know about to serve their students well.

- Williams College — located in rural Massachusetts, considered one of the top liberal arts colleges in the US, ranked number one liberal arts college several times by US News World Report's annual college rankings
- Bryn Mawr College — located in suburban Philadelphia, a "Seven Sister School," one of the top ranked women's colleges in the US
- CalTech University — located in Pasadena CA, considered by some as the top engineering research school in the world.
- Harvey Mudd College — located in Southern California, the top science and engineering liberal arts college in the US.

What's the point of having a high school counselor who doesn't spend two weeks a year to learn about schools most aren't familiar with so he can properly advise students on college options so that each individual's personality matches well with the spirit of a particular school? If he's too lazy to do his work properly — hey fucktards, read at least the annual US News college rankings so you know what is and isn't a safety school or a good match for each college bound student — should he be advising students on career and lifestyle choices? Are these the same fucktards who tell every student to go to college regardless of personal interest and test scores so a bunch of kids grow up to be broke and confused adults who wasted their most productive years getting bullshit degrees from bullshit colleges? Is bad advice that ruins people's lives what taxpayers are paying for?

Let's look at teachers: how many of them have you had who were good, who made a positive difference in your life? How many didn't make a difference at all? How many wasted your time? How many fucked you up, beat the curiosity out of you with asinine rules and demented pedagogy? Count them up. What percentage made a positive difference, is it closer to 20 percent or 80 percent? Or did they overall teach you to act, talk, and think more like a Trader Joe's cashier than the CEO you dreamed of becoming? Are you even capable of asking a question — any question — other than perfunctory ones like "how was your day?" when you're on a date, or do you mostly talk about yourself and repeat cliches because you spent a sizable chunk of your childhood in a:

...dull and ugly place, where nobody ever says anything very truthful, where everybody is playing a kind of role, as in a charade where the teachers are no more free to respond honestly to the students than the students are free to respond to the teachers or each other, where the air practically vibrates with suspicion and anxiety, the child learns to live in a daze, saving his energies for those small parts of his life that are too trivial for the adults to bother with, and thus remain his. It is a rare child who can come through his schooling with much left of his curiosity, his independence or his sense of his own dignity, competence and worth. (John Holt, published in Saturday Evening Post, 1969)

Which sounds a lot like the Boeing work environment — sub "teacher" with "manager" and "students" with "staff" — the above cited New Republic article describes. Should we be surprised that our work environments aren't much different from our school environments? Should we spend more money on replicating dysfunction and incompetence?

> [In school] I encountered authority of a different kind than I had ever encountered before, and I did not like it. And they really almost got me. They came close to really beating any curiosity out of me.
>
> — Steve Jobs

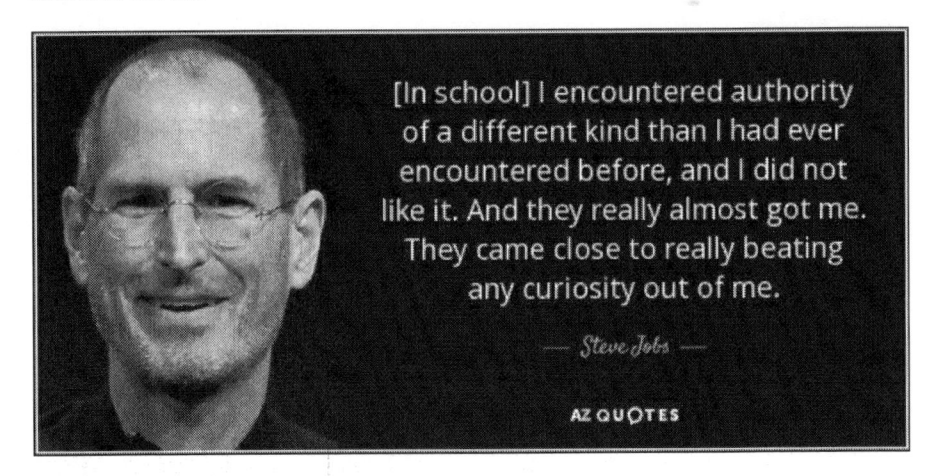

What Sort of Jobs?

Let's play along, what sort of jobs would the Federal government provide? Bernie Sanders says:

As part of the Green New Deal, we need millions of workers to rebuild our crumbling infrastructure—roads, bridges, drinking water systems, wastewater plants, rail, schools, affordable housing—and build our 100% sustainable energy system. This infrastructure is critical to a thriving, green economy.
At a time when our early childhood education system is totally inadequate, we need hundreds of thousands of workers to provide quality care to the young children of our country.
As the nation ages, we will need many more workers to provide supportive services for seniors to help them age in their homes and communities, which is where they want to be.

So does Robbie the Rapist teach four-year-olds the pledge of allegiance? Should Fat Freddie be anywhere near a shovel? What happens when Sad Sally takes care of grandma? Mickey the Methhead promises to never jerk off again while at work. The US government already provides jobs to anyone of "working age" who wants one — that's what the US military does and it's still not meeting its enlistment goals — unless he or she:

- is a psychopath

- has an iq below 82
- is obese
- is mentally or physically ill

National Center for Health Statistics at the CDC showed that 39.6% of US adults age 20 and older were obese as of 2015-2016 (37.9% for men and 41.1% for women). According to Mental Health First Aid, "in the United States, almost half of adults (46.4 percent) will experience a mental illness during their lifetime," with "half of all mental disorders [beginning] by age 14 and three-quarters by age 24." Ten percent of the population have IQs lower than 82. Let's not even bother to look up the percentage of people who are psychopaths, which I'm sure is waaaay underestimated. So are these minimum requirements for employment reasonable? Go imagine yourself having a threesome with Bernie Sanders and Elizabeth Warren if you think not. If they are, then what percentage of the US population is unemployable? Are we really going to let someone who is obese build a bridge? Or someone with an IQ lower than 82 to engineer a bridge? A chronically depressed caretaker to take care of the elderly?

Freddy wants a job. He especially likes to babysit kids.

The private and public sectors already employ many who don't meet minimum US military requirements for employment. Meaning, most of the unemployed are probably the worst of the unemployable — they can't wake up on time, they never brush their teeth, they can't remember anything that doesn't have to do with themselves, they're pathological liars, etc. And some feckless politicians still want to guarantee them jobs? It takes a highly skilled and disciplined workforce to build and repair roads and bridges — work already done by the Army Corp of Engineers by the way — you can't just let anyone have at it.

But Work Makes People Dignified
How so? According to a 2017 Gallup poll, 85% of workers in the world hate their jobs. A 2013 Forbes magazine reported that

"work is more often a source of frustration than fulfillment for nearly 90% of the world's workers." The good news is that in the US, only 70% say they hate their jobs, comparable to the percentage of American kids who say they hate mandatory education. Am I missing something, is there something dignified about hating your job? Or are the government jobs going to be so gosh darn awesome that *everyone* is going to love them and turn into the model workers champagne socialists fantasize about?

It's not a politician's job to tell people what is or isn't a dignified life, that's playing God and will lead to tyranny. And we don't force Puki the Pomeranian Princess to pull a sled in the snow to be a dignified dog. People can decide for themselves what sort of life they want to live, and for some, it's going to be a life without work. You can still have a sense of purpose in life without going to work — think of all the retired grandparents who hang out with their grandkids and tend gardens.

Puki says: "Kiya the crazy Husky can pull sleds. Me, I just want to look pretty and pampered."

Universal Basic Income
There are a lot of people who want to work but are unemployable. Like the journalist who is too lazy to fact check and too unimaginative to sense the implausibility of someone's account; doctors who don't wash their hands between patient visits; personal trainers who only talk about themselves during the entire session; Sociology professors who teach books they've never read; lawyers who don't read contracts they're paid to read.

The good news is that the next phase of automation will result in more of the unemployable employed to become unemployed. That's a good thing because it'll lead to a significant increase in productivity and — if we do it right — quality of life. Leaving a lot of people out of work, however, is a bad thing because they're likely to riot as the Luddites did in the early 19th century when their jobs were replaced by industrialization. To reduce the likelihood of widespread social disturbance and to offset the economic effects of automation, we should aim to pay everyone — yes, EVERYone in the world — a living allowance. Presidential candidate Andrew Yang's Freedom Dividend — $1000/month to every American citizen age 18-64 — is a step in that direction.

What Happens Next?
Technologically, we're so close to providing universal health care without reduction of quality and rising costs. The automation of most healthcare work will significantly reduce healthcare costs and make it and many other services accessible to everyone. This will happen sooner than later if we stop using resources to fund policies that create disasters we have to clean up and start preparing people for a future without work as we define it today. A new world is around the corner, we should see what it looks like instead of turning around and running back to 20th century solutions — guaranteed jobs and free college — to 21st century problems.

CHAPTER TWENTY SEVEN -- HOW SCHOOLS TRAIN STUDENTS TO NOT BE RESPONSIBLE

A thoughtful parent was telling me about her concerns with her elementary school aged son's academic progress. While his test scores placed him in the 97th percentile, his grades were beginning to drop and he was getting in trouble for disobedience. For instance, during the quiet reading period, he would help a classmate with vocabulary words. "He's not obedient, and I don't see why he should be," she said. "Why shouldn't he help out a classmate?"

Her son is in a system that rewards obedience and punishes responsibility. A responsible child helps a classmate. The system made it clear that obedience to rules trumps acting responsibly. (And who the fuck came up with the idea that one needs silence to read? One needs such conditions only if one believes such pedagogical rubbish. People read just fine on the subway, on buses, at the airport, etc..).

This parent was also concerned with her high school aged daughter, a good student taking honors classes. She complained that her daughter is too compliant, too obedient, too boring.

She disapproved of her daughter's approach to school work. "She just repeats whatever teacher tells her instead of problematizing an issue," she said. "I've asked her over and over again to write papers that challenge assumptions rather than accept the teacher's opinion as fact." Her daughter has been resisting her advice because "she doesn't want to get in trouble at school, she wants good grades." So she gave her daughter two options: "You can either get in trouble at school or you get in trouble at home."

This parent's daughter is also in a system that rewards obedience and punishes responsibility. Her daughter has adapted to it and she wants to make sure her son doesn't do the same.

I don't think anyone is truly comfortable with being obedient. Those who are obedient are so, or try to appear so, out of fear and habit. Yet many schools and businesses, in spite of their stated desire for innovative citizens capable to creating new paradigms, train their students and employees to be obedient, not responsible…or sentient, or compassionate, or dignified. So why the contradiction, the absurd situation? How did we get to this point?

Education reformer/activist John Gatto Taylor describing his experiences as a student and school teacher:

Consider the strange possibility that we have been deliberately taught to be irresponsible and to dislike each other for some good purpose. I am not being sarcastic or even cynical. I spent 19 years as a student, and 30 more as a school teacher and in all that time I was seldom asked to be responsible, unless you mistake obedience and responsibility for the same thing, which they certainly are not. Whether student or teacher, I gave reflective obedience to strangers for 49 years. If that isn't a recipe for irresponsibility then nothing is. In school your payoff comes from giving up your personal responsibility, just doing what you're told by strangers even if that violates the core principles of your household. There isn't any way to grow up in school, school won't let you. As I watched it happen, it takes three years to break a kid, 3 years confined to an environment of emotional neediness, songs, smiles, bright colors, cooperative games, these work much better than angry words and punishment.

Taylor doesn't consider obedience a natural state. It's a learned state — "three years to break a kid" — that's taught in school. Watch 3-4 year olds. Unless they've been coddled to the extreme, they're remarkably responsible and are constantly asking for more responsibility. By 9, these same kids will either be obedient, be either good or bad at faking obedience, or stigmatized as "special needs" for routine in-your-face disobedience, for resisting losing their freedom and individuality, for questioning why they have to learn bullshit. The obedient ones become middle-managers. The ones who fake obedience become managed staff. The "special needs" kids either become Steve Jobs or end up in jail.

Taylor on the personalities schools create:

Constant supplication for attention creates a chemistry whose products are the characteristics of modern school children — whining, treachery, dishonesty, malice, cruelty and similar traits. Ceaseless competition for attention in the dramatic fishbowl of the classroom, I have never seen this dynamic examined in the public press — not in 50 years of reading the public press. Ceaseless competition for attention in the dramatic fishbowl of the classroom, reliably delivers cowardly children, toadies, school stoolies, little people sunk into chronic boredom, little people with no apparent purpose, just like caged rats, pressing a bar for sustenance, who develop eccentric mannerisms on a periodic reinforcement schedule. Those of you who took rat psychology in college will know what I'm referring to — just like the experience of rat psychology, the bizarre behavior kids display is a function of the reinforcement schedule in the confinement of schooling to a large degree. I'm certain of that. Children like this need extensive management.

Many businesses, faced with a labor pool of needy people, reinforce what employees were taught in school instead of making the effort to teach them how to be responsible. Many businesses, faced with a consumer pool of needy people, market their products to satisfy the needs of a scared, insecure, and suspicious populace. Gatto on how schools produce consumers:

The fantastic wealth of American big business is a direct result of school training. Schools training a social lump to be needy, frightened, envious, bored, talentless and incomplete. The successful mass-production economy demands such an audience. It isn't anybody's fault. Just as the Amish small business, small farm economy requires intelligence, competence, thoughtfulness and compassion, ours needs a well managed mass — level, anxious, spiritless families, godless and conforming.

And people wonder how I can be afraid of a seemingly innocuous teenage girl but let a couple of high school drop-outs with a combined 26 felonies work on my yard and house on their own. (And pay these guys upfront and share beers with them after work). Some people think I'm crazy. I think they're the ones who are bonkers.

Taylor describing the psychological health of American consumers:

The American economy depends on schooling us that status is purchased and others run our lives. We learn there that sources of joy and accomplishment are external, that the contentment comes with the possessions, seldom from within. School cuts our ability to concentrate to a few minutes duration, creating a life-long craving for relief from boredom through outside stimulation. In conjunction with television and computer games, which employ the identical teaching methodology, these lessons are permanently inscribed. We become fearful, stupid, voiceless and addicted to novelty.

Something has to be done about the cultural malaise that's

destroying America. If schools won't change their approach to teaching students, then businesses need to invest the time to teach employees responsibility. It may turn out that the time and money invested in teaching responsibility and unlearning obedience may better serve the long-term interest of businesses.

The toughest part of building a business and new brand isn't taxes (which are annoying and sometimes absurd), it's human resources. When we started, our labor pool was limited to teens because those who are qualified aren't willing to take a chance on a new business. Many applied and I was shocked at how incompetent, irresponsible, and obedient (or bad at faking obedience) they were. So now we identify candidates we think are willing to unlearn what they learned in school and then develop them into responsible, thoughtful, confident, and dignified contributors.

CHAPTER TWENTY EIGHT -- HOW TO BREAK RULES AND GET AWAY WITH IT

Conversation with an employee:

"Call him a Fuckface," I demanded.

"I will not. This is wrong!"

"DO IT. CALL HIM A FUCKFACE!!!"

I DON'T WANT TO!" How about I call him monkey turd instead, please?"

"No, he deserves to be called a Fuckface. DO IT!"

After some more back and forth, she relented and called the customer "Fuckface." Customer left a $5 tip on a $12 bill.

For those wondering what a Fuckface looks like:

We'll get back to the Fuckface incident later. There's a point to it.

How to Turn Someone into a Fucked-Up Fuckface

While American schools and society *tells* people to break rules and challenge conventions — "to think outside the box" (dorkiest phrase of the century) — it paradoxically *trains* people to follow rules and to be conventional. Somewhere Michel Foucault calls this the most effective form of mind control: let people think they're special when in fact they're just another fuckface. In any case, those who don't know how to break and test rules will either:

a) find it difficult to get ahead because they've turned into dumbasses.
b) look like dumbasses while breaking rules.
c) break the wrong rules too many times.
d) think of breaking rules as a guilty pleasure, turning something as mundane as eating chocolate into a subliminally kinky act.

If you're interested in why schools teach obedience to rules, check out former New York state Teacher of the Year and education activist John Taylor Gatto's Underground History of American Education, and Against School. For our purposes here, I'm more interested in the sort of people such an environment produces. Gatto on obedience expected from teachers and students:

Consider the strange possibility that we have been deliberately taught to be irresponsible and to dislike each other for some good purpose. I am not being sarcastic or even cynical. I spent 19 years as a student, and 30 more as a school teacher and in all that time I was seldom asked to be responsible, unless you mistake obedience and responsibility for the same thing, which they certainly are not. Whether student or teacher, I gave reflective obedience to strangers for 49 years. If that isn't a recipe for irresponsibility then nothing is. In school your payoff comes from giving up your personal responsibility, just doing what you're told by strangers even if that violates the core principles of your household. There isn't any way to grow up in school, school won't let you. As I watched it happen, it takes three years to break a kid, 3 years confined to an environment of emotional neediness, songs, smiles, bright colors, cooperative games, these work much better than angry words and punishment.

Gatto claims that children ARE naturally responsible, that at school their sense of responsibility is beaten out of them — "it takes three years to break a kid." Gatto on the type of students such schools produce:

Constant supplication for attention creates a chemistry whose products are the characteristics of modern school children — whining, treachery, dishonesty, malice, cruelty and similar traits. Ceaseless competition for attention in the dramatic fishbowl of the classroom, I have never seen this dynamic examined in the public press — not in 50 years of reading the public press. Ceaseless competition for attention in the dramatic fishbowl of the classroom, reliably delivers cowardly children, toadies, school stoolies, little people sunk into chronic boredom, little people with no apparent purpose, just like caged rats, pressing a bar for sustenance, who develop eccentric mannerisms on a periodic reinforcement schedule. Those of you who took rat psychology in college will know what I'm referring to — just like the experience of rat psychology, the bizarre behavior kids display is a function of the reinforcement schedule in the confinement of schooling to a large degree. I'm certain of that. Children like this need extensive management.

Most schools turn most kids into fuck-ups and most of them will look like fuckfaces as adults, impatiently waiting for their next paycheck so they can purchase novelties and escapes — orgasm orgasm orgasm! — that will dull the pain and boredom of their everyday lives. Again, boredom isn't a natural state, it's learned. Contrast this with Amish education, which *formally* ends in 8th grade. Gatto again:

Look at Johns Hopkins University, not one of my favorite universities, but they've been tracking the Amish for a long time. They've published several...mind blowing books about what has happened in Amish America. In this century, at the beginning of the century, there were 5000 of these people, now there are 150,000. So the group itself has retained its integrity and grown 30 times. Second, 100% of the Amish, or as close to that as humanly possible, has independent livelihoods, and its divided 50% in small entrepreneurial businesses and 50% in small farms. Now consider the drawbacks these people labor under – the government of Pennsylvania has been their sworn enemy through the century. And, they don't use telephones, they don't use computers, they don't use cars, and they go to the 8th grade only because the Supreme Court cut a deal with them in 1976. So with all these drawbacks you have a community that with all intents and purposes has no crime at all, that takes care of old and young because it mixes both of those groups together in the life of the community, is amazingly successful, amazingly wealthy, and amazingly unschooled!

The Amish are neither fuck-ups nor fuckfaces. They don't need to be micromanaged, they're self-sufficient, self-reliant, and productive. The Amish community is capitalism as Adam Smith had hoped it'd be in practice, without the corruption, the oligarchic excesses, and the concentrations of capital and power.

How Amish Break Rules

Those who think that the Amish are slavish rule followers and brainwashed screwballs probably also think Dead Poet's Society is a highbrow film about stifled creativity finally unleashed. "Rip it out, rip it out!" we're exhorted by a renegade English teacher who fashions himself as Walt Whitman's "O Captain, My [Fucking] Captain." Then meet up in a cave to write poetry that channels someone's metaphoric cock into some naifs hands, hopefully leading to some action with some real, public school pussy. The narcissist watching Dead Poet's of course projects, identifies with the "courageous rule breaking boys." But that's a ploy, a trick to get the audience to think they're in on some juicy highbrow acts of courage, acts of love, when all the boys are doing is what they have always been doing: jerking off. Instead of using their hands, they use contrived and sentimental poetry; instead of a blow up doll or a watermelon, they have that girl from the other side of the tracks. It's the same shit, different form. It's a movie about how boys "break rules" by hiding their porno mags and jerk off sessions from scoundrel faculty, except the porn is dressed up as poetry and the jerk off sessions don't include pizza to be eaten by the new kid, so enough people will find the film highbrow enough, inspirational enough to win bullshit awards that confirm some fucked up prejudices. No wonder Robin Williams named Dead Poet's his most embarrassing film.

Dead Poet's isn't unusual, similar formula is used over and over again to secure enough character identification to make a film profitable, perhaps memorable within public consciousness. Like Good Will Hunting, same shit, except they flip the script. Instead of preppy boys, now we're supposed to be down with the bros. Or Twilight, where girl next door is sandwiched between high society vampires and low society beasts. Daddy doesn't approve of either, and that's precisely why it's every middle-class white girl's fantasy.

Point is, while we're told by pop culture — music, film, books, Oprah!, even CNN — to break the rules, we're trained to follow them, however inane they may be. Which results in some fucked up confused people. "I am Good Will Hunting," fantasizes the kid with intellectual pretentions and no chance of going anywhere with his degrees in Anthropology, English Literature, and Women's Studies. "I am Robin Williams," imagines the teacher who jerks off to kiddie porn and asks students to write personal narratives. Fantasy and narcissism is what we're left with when there's no guidance, only glib exhortations.

Amish society doesn't preach obedience. They are, after all, the ones with the courage to tell the government to fuck off. They teach their members to think about how to handle temptations as sentient INDIVIDUALS, and not as preposterous film characters. That's why Amish guidelines (not rules) are purposely UNWRITTEN and Amish governance is so decentralized that each church can make its own rules (based on guidelines). That's why Amish teens are given the opportunity to explore the "outside" world — booze, smokes, jewelry, Oprah, make-up, whatever it is they could not have — and then asked to make a decision. Those who return are baptized, their convictions finally deep enough for the experience. They're asked to break the rules to understand them. Godspeed to those few who leave.

The Rule Breakers

Anderson Cooper, despite his Yale degree and his blue blood lineage (Vanderbilt), had to forge his first press pass because nobody wanted to hire and sponsor him. Steve Jobs and Steve Wozniak figured out a way to get free long distance. Bill Gates rigged the computer system to give himself free computer time and his preferred class schedule. John F. Kennedy blew up toilets while in high school. They didn't break the rules for guilty pleasure, or as narcissistic announcement of the self. There's a greater goal, a higher purpose. Anderson wanted a chance and made one for himself. The Steves wanted to know if they can take on big corporations. Bill needed more computer time to figure out what he can do with them. JFK, eh, he probably was being being a narcissistic douchebag, but experience must have been useful while he handled the Cuban Missile Crisis.

How to Call Someone a Fuckface and Get Away With It

Most of our applicants are either good or bad at faking obedience, or simply obedient. (There's a lot of repression going around). Neither are acceptable in our work culture. It'll zap the life out of them, they'll turn into the caged rats Gatto describes above, if they're not already there. They need to be reprogrammed. They need to stop thinking of themselves as the main characters of some sappy action film.

To beat obedience out of new employees, we have them practice doing what they've been told to never do. AND get rewarded for doing so (big tips). Totally Pavlovian. We offer Bad Service for $1. "Includes a finger and customer choice of being called a Fuckface, Monkey Dick, or Gorilla Jizz." Most can't pull it off at first, or do so with hilarious results. That's a good sign, as many of those who can do so see it as an opportunity to express narcissistic rage.

The point of this rite of passage ISN'T to create sassy bitchy employees. The point is to get employees to think about the wants and needs of the customer in a way they never have before (like, who would ever order Bad Service? Well, people do, so there, stop projecting); to become comfortable with being uncomfortable; to recognize that rules are meant to maintain artificial order at the expense of individual responsibility and dignity; to test and break the rules so they can finally see the point of them and perhaps, one day, change them for the better.

CHAPTER TWENTY NINE -- ALIVE JUICE BAR PRINCIPLES

Employees are expected to internalize these principles.

Cook with your senses. Quality assurance. Our products must smell, look, and feel right. This is our last line of defense against bad products. Those who cook solely according to process and recipes are much more likely to miss a piece of rancid meat or spoiled ginger. Those who cook with their senses will have the instinct to notice when something is wrong.

You're not special until someone you'll never meet says you are. Guard against inflated self-esteem, which distorts reality, weakens work ethic, and thins skin.

It's your fault (especially when it isn't). Don't make excuses, don't play victim, and don't allow others to think of themselves as victims. Those who are mentally tough enough to be responsible for everything that goes on in the world will be empowered to change the world. The rest assume they can't do anything about it. Don't tolerate anyone who plays victim.

Never say "No" to a customer. "No" creates a communication barrier. Always maintain a we-can-do-it-all atmosphere. Figure out a way to provide what the customer wants.

We always have what the customer wants (even when we don't). If you understand what the customer is really wants, you'll be able to sell him/her something, regardless of initial request.

Ask questions, question everything. Smart people are aware of how little they know. Dumb people think they know it all, so they rarely ask questions and mostly make trite and misinformed proclamations. We learn by asking good questions, not by memorizing processes. Ask customers questions to understand their needs and preferences. Question how things are done to understand and improve processes.

Be skeptical, not suspicious. Skepticism is based on reality. Suspicion is based on cynicism and prejudice. Never allow yourself to believe what you want to believe.

Be responsible, not obedient. Being obedient is not the same as being responsible. Obedience breeds immaturity, ennui, fear, and a tendency to follow pointless and infantalizing rules and traditions. Only those who take responsibility for everything that happens in the world live meaningful, dignified lives.

Be charming, not polite. It's easy to be polite. Just follow etiquette, repeat till you're in a zombie state. Polite people are petty, innocuous, and unoriginal. They're also boring and insincere. Charm requires effort — understanding the customer as an individual — (brutal) honesty, social risks, sincerity, and care.

Don't be afraid to make mistakes. Learn from your mistakes, don't shy away from calculated risk, and don't be afraid of failure.

You'll never be good enough. "Success is a lousy teacher. It makes smart people think they can't lose." — Bill Gates

PART IV -- CUSTOMERS

It's better to be feared than loved...
  -- Machiavelli

CHAPTER THIRTY -- HOW TO TALK TO CUSTOMERS

Talk to them as a courtesan would to her benefactor. Or you could talk to them as some street skank whore does to her john; or as some $300/hour escort to her client. Think about the differences between the three:

Whore: fucks a lot of guys each day to get her drugs.

Escort: fucks a few guys and listens to them complain about stupid shit a few times a week to pay for living expenses and a few luxuries.

Courtesan: fucks a few guys per year she advises on marital, political and business matters.

Which do you want to be? You want your customers to be benefactors, clients, or johns? You want to live in a world where there's a good chance someone's going to knock your rotting teeth out or where you don't have to worry about being murdered on the job? Do you want to live a life where your opinion matters? So you better start practicing now because the courtesans have been working on their game ever since they could talk and walk.

What's the only difference between a street whore and an escort? The former has a drug habit for way too long. What's the difference between an escort and a courtesan? The former is a narcissist. Notice I haven't mentioned anything about looks because as long as the body's bangin', that's mostly irrelevant.

Know Your Customer

What do most people like to talk about the most? Pick:

a) Ideas
b) Other people
c) Themselves

Correct answer is C. Narcissism is our Original Sin and your job is to figure out how to curb your own narcissistic urges so you can turn the customer into your benefactor (what most want to be) instead of a john (what most are). Put simply, your job is to seduce those we want as customers and to repel the shitheads.

Pick:

a) Treat others as you want to be treated
b) Treat others as they treat you
c) Treat others as they want to be treated

Those who pick A are intolerant narcissists because they project their wants and needs onto other people, they don't realize that other people have different preferences and perspectives from their own. Those who pick A can only have friends who are copies of themselves because any deviance from their narrow worldview offends their sense of self and righteousness. Repel these people, they're dangerous. They color themselves with righteous sounding identities such as "social justice warrior" and "human rights activist" to hide the fact that they're totalitarians and liars.

If you picked B, then you've picked up on psychological mirroring, which is how you achieve "greater connection and understanding with the individual who is being mirrored" (Wiki entry of Mirroring). Mirroring requires empathy, which is not the same as sympathy (ie. narcissists being nice), and empathy involves seeing something from different perspectives. Those who pick B are also good at protecting themselves from being used because they give off vibe that they will retaliate in kind to protect themselves.

Those who pick C are capable of empathy, but incapable of protecting themselves.

How to Talk to Customers

Now that you know who the shitheads are — they often refuse to follow Ordering Guidelines because they wrongly assume employees are as easily stressed out as they are (narcissistic projection) — you can focus on providing the best service possible to our customers without violating your integrity. All prostitutes have boundaries.

Ask Them Questions

Two to three is best, any more and some get annoyed. When you ask someone a question about themselves, you make that person feel less lonely. Most are very lonely because most people prefer to talk about themselves than ask questions, which means few are listening. (Hermits, ironically, are the least lonely because they haven't lost the ability — a rich inner world — to keep themselves company). A customer you make feel less lonely becomes your benefactor. It's not hard to pull off. Here's an example of an uncivilized conversation:

You: Whom did you vote for?
Customer: Trump
You: You're an ignorant racist!
Customer: Hey fuck you.

Never rush to judgment and conclusion, you'll never learn and grow if you do that. Here's how to have the same conversation the civilized way.

You: Whom did you vote for?

Customer: Trump
You: Why did you vote for him?
Customer: I like that he wants to get the US out of foreign engagements we have no business being in and I like that he promises to protect the US steel industry because that's a matter of national security. We need to have a robust steel industry in case we go to war...
You: Interesting, I never thought of it that way, thanks for the insight. Do you think Trump is a racist?
Customer: Not anymore than any of the other candidates. He's just more uncensored and I care more about results than insults.

Always ask at least 2 follow up questions. (Again, too many and you'll annoy some people so watch for that). The more questions you ask, the closer you'll get to the truth. Another uncouth conversation:

You: How are you?
Customer: I'm fine. How are you?
You: Omigod, my math professor is such a stupid jerk off. Can you believe he doesn't give partial credit? Who does that? I mean, I'm really good at Math, I got straight As in it in high school and now I have a C. How is that possible? Don't you think there's something wrong with him?

That's how skanks talk — mostly about themselves and their own stupid problems. Few people care about your problems. Some will pretend to care. An escort, for instance, talks to show solidarity with her customer. Example:

Customer: my son is having a lot of problems at school.
You: I'm sorry. Boys are really tough to deal with at that age. He'll grow out of it, I'm sure.

A courtesan, on the other hand, talks to solve other people's problems. Example:

Customer: my son is having a lot of problems at school.
You: What sort of problems?

Customer: drugs, not doing his schoolwork. He's close to flunking out.
You: Why is he doing those things?
Customer: Not sure. He could be bored, he doesn't learn the way they want him to learn.
You: Would you consider a boarding school that's better suited for his learning style?
Customer: Maybe. Tell me more...

This conversation gives customers an opportunity to get beyond ranting, to think about solutions to his problem. The courtesan's value is in her usefulness, not her sex.

Avoid Banalities and Cliches
Make yourself stand out. If everyone else is asking: "Hi, how are you?" then find another question to ask. "Where are you going?," for instance. Example:

You: Where are you going after this?
Customer: Checking out a wedding venue.
You: You getting married?
Customer: Yes!
You: Do you have a caterer?
Customer: No, why do you ask?
You: We've catered weddings. Can we put a bid in?
Customer: Absolutely!

Asking people *what* they're doing will generate more business and social opportunities. Another example:

You: What do you do for work?
Customer: I'm a structural engineer.
You: Hey, I'm majoring in Physics to become a structural engineer. Do you have internships?
Customer: We do. Have a resume ready by Friday and I'll stop in to look at it.
You: Awesome, will do. Thanks!

See why some people have all the luck? These people live a different routine from those who have no luck or bad luck. You're responsible for your own karma.

Don't Lie to the Customer

Your goal is to build trust. Flattery, even when it makes the customer feel good, will break down trust.

Say "I don't know."
That's what intelligent people say when they don't know something. Only broken, insecure people with inflated self-esteem make random guesses. These people are more concerned with how they look than the truth and they end up looking good only to those who can't help them move ahead.

It's ok to guess as long as you let the customer know that you're making an educated guess.

Never Say What You Don't Mean
Even when a customer says hi to you with an insincere and trite greeting — "How are you?" — don't just play along to be polite — "I'm fine, thank you. How are you?" — if that's not how you feel. Compulsive lying begins with seemingly benign little lies. Batshit crazy also begins with thinking that everything needs to be A-ok all the fucking time and with suppressing your emotions. Engaging in scripted politeness will also train you to NOT listen when people talk. Don't let these savages destroy your life. Alternative responses to the vapid "How are you?" question:

- "Dunno, haven't thought about it." (This one elicits the most laughs)
- "Why do you ask?"
- Ignore the question. (What I usually do)

Or answer honestly. It could be "I'm fine." Could also be:

- "I'm angry. I want to beat the shit out of someone."
- "I'm really confused because my boyfriend told me

something last night that came out of nowhere yada yada yada...."

Don't let customers violate your integrity. Don't lie about stupid shit because if you do, you'll soon start lying about all sorts of shit out of habit.

Be Precise and Say Less
The more you say, the less people will understand and trust you. Say only what needs to be said. Say what you have to say in as few words as possible to minimize misunderstanding and sounding like a rambling idiot. Example:

Customer: What do you do with the juice fiber?
Bad Answer: Well, we generally just throw out most of it. Some of it though we'll use to make the raw carrot cake desert. We'll also use it in the avocado salad.

Good Answer: (pointing to fridge) Carrot cake and avocado salads.

The good answer will result in more customers exploring other products. Bad answer will confuse most customers. Keep it simple. Less is more, less is more.

Control Customer Perception and Expectations

Customer perception and expectations are as important as the products themselves. It's similar to psychological framing:

The framing effect is an example of cognitive bias, in which people react to a particular choice in different ways depending on how it is presented...

Much of the perception and expectations are framed by the decor, prices, and online marketing (yelp reviews, Facebook updates). You frame it by how you describe our products.

Never use superlatives — "tastes incredible" — to describe our products. Taste is subjective so that's for the customer to decide. Just describe the flavor and texture profile of a product.

Reference familiar flavors and textures if that helps. Examples:

Bad: "The Supermodel tastes great and will make you look like a Supermodel, guaranteed!"

Good: Probably won't make you a Supermodel. But you'll feel like one: mildly hungry, bitchy, and jaded. You'll understand why Naomi Campbell throws phones at people." (description on menu).

Those who order the Supermodel often comment on how it's a lot more filling than they expected.

Play the slow game. Be modest, never boastful. It'll make our products taste better. The sales will come.

Be Dignified

If a customer treats you poorly, it's your fault not the customer's. Only undignified people blame others when treated poorly. The dignified blame themselves and take steps to ensure it never happens again.

This is difficult to pull off because most American schools and much of American society train people to play victim. Society even celebrates victims, as Nietzsche predicted it would (slave morality). Avoid the temptation to play victim, it'll dis-empower you. Be noble, not pathetic. From our application question, pick what you think most people pick:

Someone mugs you. Whose fault is it that you were mugged?
a) Mugger's fault
b) Your fault
c) Society's fault

Leftist Lemmings pick C. Kookie Conservatives pick A. Noble people pick B. The moment you think like a victim is the moment you lose control of your destiny and become a victim. The predators can smell a prey who deserves to be eaten.

Be Commanding

If you can tell that a customer doesn't like something, *command* them to return it and fix it to their liking. Don't ask them if they want you to fix it because they would've asked you to do so already if they're well adjusted adults. No, you're dealing with cowards who prefer childish lies: "no, it's fine" (usually the problem is that it's too green tasting) when it's not because they think it's rude to say otherwise. So you have to *command* them to do what's best for them, treat them like the children they are. Say "bring it here, I'll fix it." And resist the urge to call that person a "passive-aggressive fucktard" as you fix the problem.

CHAPTER THIRTY ONE -- OBEDIENT VERSUS RESPONSIBLE

From Alive Juice Bar's Guidelines, Principles, and Values:

Be responsible, not obedient. Being obedient is not the same as being responsible. Obedience breeds immaturity, ennui, fear, and a tendency to follow pointless and infantalizing rules and traditions. Only those who take responsibility for everything that happens in the world live meaningful, dignified lives.

We train obedience out of our employees. They're expected to be responsible, not obedient. Obedient people — often trained to be so at schools, work, and home — are incapable of being responsible.

The obedient employee obeys the customer and will give her whatever she orders. But sometimes giving the customer what they order isn't the same as giving the customer what they want, a good experience. The obedient employee will not assume responsibility if the customer doesn't like what she ordered — "it's not my fault, she ordered it, I just did what she told me to do." The responsible employee assumes full responsibility for customer experience and is much more likely to ask additional questions to ensure the customer has a positive experience. Responsible employees treat customers as individuals. Obedient employees don't give a shit about anyone but themselves.

Obedient versus Responsible

New Customer: I've heard kale smoothies are good for me. I'd like a kale smoothie (one of our more bitter drinks).
Obedient Employee: Sure thing. Here it is. Hope you like it.
New Customer: (sips) Interesting. (Doesn't like it).

versus

New Customer: I've heard kale smoothies are good for me. I'd like a kale smoothie.
Responsible Employee: Do you have a sweet tooth?
New Customer: (slightly embarrassed)Mmm, yes, a bit.
Responsible: That's ok. Do you like pineapple?
New Customer: I love pineapple.
Responsible: Great, then I recommend the Green Margarita. It's a sweeter version of the kale smoothie because it has pineapple, which is good for you.
New Customer: I'll take that then.
Responsible: I'll get that started for you. Just want to make sure you have a good first experience here. Here's your Green Margarita. How do you like it?
New Customer: It's sooo good. Thank you so much.

The responsible employee asks the customer questions, three in example above. Responsible employees have a higher ask-to-talk ratio than do obedient employees, who mostly repeat (often without understanding) whatever authority figure tells them.

Obedient employees will do whatever they're told to do because they're afraid of responsibility. Responsible employees are constantly concerned about how they impact other people because they're prepared to assume fault for anything that happens. Responsible employees ask questions such as "are you sure we should make kale chips even though there are only 2 heads of kale left?" Obedient employees will make kale chips as told, even if it means the next shift won't have any kale for drinks.

This is why we ask so many questions, esp. to new customers. We satisfy the customer by getting to know them better, not by obeying them (customer is sometimes wrong policy). This is also why many regular customers let us customize their drinks and meals. They trust that we know them well enough to provide for them.

CHAPTER THIRTY TWO -- WHAT IS MEANS TO BE RESPONSIBLE

Being responsible means NOT being obedient. Restaurants like Red Robin are obedient to their customers, giving them what they want, whether it's bottomless fries or coke. Who cares if the customer is diabetic, it's what he wants. So give it to him! These restaurants hire friendly and agreeable servers who don't ask questions and simply get their jobs done and bills paid.

Juice bars should be different. (Unfortunately, some of them aren't). Juice bars are unlike conventional restaurants because their purpose isn't solely to entertain the customer, but also to guide them about health and diet matters. Responsible juice bars build trust rather than give into customer demands for the latest health fad. That's difficult to do because most schools train students to be obedient instead of responsible workers.

An applicant chose "I work hard because I have a lot of responsibilities" on our questionnaire. I asked her what she's responsible for. Her response mentioned school, some other mumbo jumbo. I asked her if she has children. Nope. Mortgage? Nope. Ailing parents in need of income and care? Nope. A dog, any pets? Nope. I hope she's an outlier, not representative of most in her age group. If she is representative, we've raised a generation of people, who, after being praised for tying their shoes, counting to nine, winning third place (out of three competitors), getting a B, getting up in the morning — for breathing — may be incapable of ever becoming responsible. It's too much work, the strain of thinking about the wants and needs of others would break them. It's easier to follow the rules, or at least pretend to follow the rules. Smile, be friendly and agreeable enough so nobody eats me is how they will survive in this dog-eat-dog world.

Children are naturally responsible and resilient. Watch 5 year olds. Most enjoy responsibility and are constantly asking for more. These kids at age 10 will, after years of schooling and propaganda about the "proper" and "ideal" childhood, become obedient, or, more often, bad at faking obedience. They've lost their natural state, their resilience and sense of responsibility. They've been taught that work sucks, that it's distinct from leisure, that education only happens in school, and they should "enjoy" their childhood by being as idle and free of responsibility as they can because adulthood and being responsible is going to suck. No wonder so many people grow up to hate work. No wonder so many young adults are unprepared for work. They've never been trained to be responsible, nor do they find responsibility enjoyable.

Certainly, they've been told that being responsible is a virtue, just as they have been repeatedly told to "work hard," "be confident," "think positive," "work hard," "be friendly," "be responsible," "do your best," "work hard," "be polite," and so forth. Telling someone to do this and be that isn't enough. They most likely will understand whatever you're telling them in the abstract, and experience "working hard" or "doing your best" solely as a subjective feeling (I feel that I'm working hard therefore I am working hard), never measured against objective reality (I must not work hard because everyone around me works much longer hours). They don't have anything to measure their experience against.

Here's a story I tell my employees. A boy announced to his mother that he had received a 100 percent on his test. Insecure and immature, his motivation was to receive praise from his mother, who would only praise him if he received a perfect store, anything less was unacceptable. This time, he didn't receive praise. His mother asked "why didn't you get a 110?"

"There's no extra credit on this test," replied the boy.

"Stop making excuses and blaming other people," snapped the mother. "Grow up and take responsibility for your failures."

"But there's no extra credit on this test," the boy shot back. "You're asking me to do the impossible!" This is crazy.

"You're the one who is crazy. And lazy, stupid, immature, irresponsible. Figure out how to get 110. FIGURE IT OUT!" demanded the mother.

The boy went to his room, frustrated and confused, nearly in tears.

The next test didn't have any extra credit questions either. So he wrote his own extra credit question, which he answered correctly. Being lazy, he didn't put much thought into the question. And the teacher ignored his attempt to improve his score, probably thinking he's another annoying grade grubber.

He continued to write extra credit questions. Finally, after several tries, the teacher gave him an extra 5 points because he asked a well thought out question, a question so good she presented to the class to discuss.

He never did get the 110 his mother demanded from him. But this 105 score boosted his confidence far more than any praise he'd ever received from his mother. The experience also taught him that anything is possible, that making excuses and blaming other people for one's failures is what limits creative thinking.

This experience didn't make him responsible. He continued to make excuses and blame others for his failures. But the experience served as a reminder of what's possible in life when one is responsible.

CHAPTER THIRTY THREE -- NEVER SAY "NO" TO A CUSTOMER

Never say "No" to a customer. "No" creates a communication barrier. Always maintain a we-can-do-it-all atmosphere. Figure out a way to provide what the customer wants.

This policy is similar to restauranteur Cameron Mitchell's "The Answer is Yes. What's the Question" policy.

Milkshake Story

Mitchell was celebrating his son's birthday at a restaurant. His son wants a chocolate milkshake so they ask the server for one. Server tells them that they don't *offer* milkshakes.

Mitchell asks, "Do you have milk? Do you have chocolate ice cream? Do you have a blender? Well, you can make a chocolate milkshake." The server asks the manager, but the answer is the same: no milkshake because it's not on the menu.

The answer was "no" because the server and manager were obedient, not responsible . They followed rules because they were afraid to make and to take responsibility for their mistakes. As long as they follow the rules, they can blame someone else if the customer doesn't have a good experience.

Ultimately, executive management is to blame for Mitchell's bad experience. They're the ones who set company guidelines and policies and oversee training of floor staff. Their leadership failed to give employees the confidence to be responsible and make thoughtful decisions.

Someone told Mitchell that the exact same thing had happened to him—at one of Mitchell's own restaurants. That infuriated Mitchell. He has since made sure that every new employee hears the "Milkshake Story" first day of training. "We want our people to have the attitude, 'The answer is yes. What's the question?'" he says. This simple philosophy is one of the reasons Mitchell's restaurants take regular customers and turn them into raving fans.

Our "Say No to No" policy isn't just about producing thoughtful and responsible employees, it's about creating an atmosphere where customers feel like they can talk to and trust us. Early on, we noticed many customers shutting down or becoming angry whenever we told them "no."

New Customer: Do you have strawberries?
Obedient Employee: No, we don't.
New Customer: Oh, ok. Do you have blueberries?
Obedient Employee: Nope.
New Customer: Ok. I'll stop by some other time.

Versus responsible employee

New Customer: Do you have strawberries?
Responsible Employee: We're seasonal so we'll have them soon. Are you looking for something fruity?
New Customer: Mmmm, yeah.
Responsible Employee: Do you like mangoes because they smell and look great today?
New Customer: Yeah, I like mangoes.
Responsible Employee: How about the Tropical Bugs bunny. It has mangoes, pineapple, banana and a bit of carrot juice, which brings out the mango and pineapple flavors.
New Customer: Okay, I'll take that.

Responsible Employee: How is it?
New Customer: So good. Thank you!

Responsible employees have a higher ask-to-talk ratio. Asking questions invites customer to talk, to work with the barista to come up with something that will make her happy. Another example:

Customer: Do you sell milkshakes?
Obedient: No, sorry.
Customer: Oh, ok.

versus responsible.

Customer: Do you sell milkshakes?
Responsible: We have something better and tastes just like it. Would you like to try it?
Customer: What's it called? What's in it?
Responsible: It's an avocado milkshake. It has avocado, peanut butter, some kale, and your choice of fruit — I recommend apple — and whey protein. It tastes just like a milkshake but it's so much healthier, guaranteed.
Customer: Hmmm, ok. I'll try it.
Responsible: Great...here you go.
Customer: Omigosh, it really is like a milkshake! Thank you so much!!!

Responsible employee understands the customer isn't ordering a milkshake, he's asking for a feeling. He wants something — taste, texture, maybe color — that will remind him of happy times, perhaps memorable childhood events. The milkshake is irrelevant. A good barista will be able to recreate the milkshake, give him the feeling he wants guilt-free.

It's tough to get "no" out of our vocabulary. We all still make the mistake of saying "no" to a customer. But all employees know there are other, more positive ways, to say "no." It just requires some thought.

CHAPTER THIRTY FOUR -- HOW NOT TO RUN A START UP BUSINESS

I received an email from someone wanting to open a raw food/juice bar in a small Montana town. She asked six juice bars from around the country to provide her a couple of drink recipes. Excerpt of her email:

"A few years ago I attended Allisa Cohen's raw food teacher training program, and last summer, I spent a month studying at the Matthew Kenney raw food academy in Oklahoma. In spite of my familiarity with raw food, I am heightenedly nervous about providing juices and smoothies that my Montana customers will like."

She lacks confidence in her cooking skills because, in spite of her (likely useless, counterproductive) raw food education, she doesn't know how to cook. She can probably follow recipes, but she can't cook, at least not for a restaurant. First paragraph of my response:

"But you live in a different region. You're dealing with a different set of suppliers, prices, ingredients, palates, etc. Unless cost is irrelevant (people are willing to pay anything for your products), or you have a sophisticated supply chain and food preservation system (like what Subway, Evolution Fresh, Jamba Juice have), you can't be using recipes from different parts of the country. Food business doesn't

work like that (unless you have a sophisticated supply chain...). I saw a juice bar fall apart immediately because the owner thought she could use her favorite home recipes at work. So she ended up with one drink made with red grapes, another with green grapes... too complicated and fussy. Doing it this way, she had to price each drink differently and made produce shopping and employee training a nightmare."

In other words, I told her that she doesn't have the right attitude and mindset to run a start-up restaurant that's trying to introduce a new concept to the community. Nor is she focusing on the important issues. Anyone who thinks running a successful restaurant is primarily about having the "right" recipes and friendly service should not open an unbranded restaurant — they'll likely be crushed within a month. These are the people who think that grandma's meatloaf recipe, if just given a chance, will make a million bucks and make grandma famous (I've been offered several recipes that will supposedly make me "a million bucks"). These people think running a restaurant is like hosting a 12 person dinner party, that the only difference is scale.

So what does it take to run a start up restaurant that's introducing a new concept and brand? Here are a few guidelines I've learned to follow.

The product is secondary, even irrelevant

Ever wonder how restaurants survive, even thrive, despite shitty food? For instance, I've wondered about 13 Coins, Jade Garden, Buca Di Beppo and many others. Or why restaurants that serve extraordinary food don't survive? The reason why we're surrounded mostly by bad to mediocre food is because the quality of the product is secondary, and sometimes it's irrelevant.

So how do restaurants get people to pay for, over and over again, shitty food sometimes paired with ridiculous decor and irresponsible service? In some cases, they get away with it because that's what their core customers are accustomed to and ultimately, taste is subjective. People are creatures of habit, and if microwaved pizza is what's eaten everyday for the past 20 years, that's what they'll probably eat for the rest of their lives, even if they hate it and know there's better pizza available. Other restaurants, like Hooters and Buca Di Beppo, distract customers away from the food with kitsch. Some Chinese restaurants lure customers with mounds of comfort food at low prices. 13 Coins thrives by attracting those who are either too tired or drunk to give a shit (open 24 hours), or are impressed with exorbitant prices and faux upscale decor in diner settings.

People make choices about food based on the interplay of emotions, perceptions and rationalizations. There's peer pressure, there's yearning for childhood memories, there are negotiations of social identity, there's the comfort of habit. There's fear of the unknown, of pain, and of failure. There's confusion about which "expert" is right and who is wrong. There may be subconscious desire for self-destruction, eating junk food as a slow, hedonistic death. Most decisions aren't made based on objective standard and quality of food (taste is subjective, but quality isn't).

The point is, it's not the product that sells, it's the hopes, aspirations, values, and lifestyle the product represents that people are purchasing. That's why it's more productive to focus on controlling customer expectations, building and managing supply chain and workflow processes, training employees, and refining business vision and culture than to worry about recipes and products.

Control customer expectations

I once watched a restaurant describe itself, when it opened, in glowing terms, comparing itself to famous fine dining restaurants around the world. Customers, expecting fine dining experience on par with Per Se and French Laundry, were disappointed. This restaurant failed, not because of shitty food—the food was solid. It failed because it wasn't able to meet expectations. That's why it's considered crass to brag about oneself—it'll get you in trouble.

We have extremely high expectations for ourselves but we don't go around telling everyone that we're the bomb, or that we're something we're not. It's the customer's job to grade us and tell us what they think of us.

Control customer perception

Often, there's a mismatch between what your business is (or is trying to be) and how customers perceive it. Most people judge a book by its cover and think they already know, without asking questions, researching, and controlling for bias, what other people are about, their motivations and aspirations. These are the same people who will think they know what a restaurant is about without even studying its menu. Or they'll make assumptions about operating hours without fact checking it online or in person. They may think they already know what's on the menu, how everything is prepared, and why the owner opened the business. That's the way the world is, you have to assume that people don't think you're special enough for them to devote time to get to know you. No use in complaining about it, just work on making yourself important to others by building trust and being responsible for them.

It takes effort to change how people think about you and your business. But it can be done as long as you're persistent and don't mind being repetitive. Small and large established businesses have to deal with wrong perceptions. For instance, UPS has been working on correcting perception that they only deliver packages, even though that's a small part of their product and service offerings.

At Alive Juice Bar, employees control new customer perception the moment he walks into the door. Every second counts, as new customers can form opinions about a business in fewer than three seconds. It's difficult to change someone's opinion, so we get their attention the moment they enter the business in order to control how customers perceive the business. Getting a new customer's attention like this invites them to ask more questions and to build a relationship with your business.

Build products around the existing utilities infrastructure

If you don't have enough funds to build your ideal store, let the utilities infrastructure and refrigeration units determine products and recipes. You need to make sure that you have the bins and storage space for ingredients used to build products. (Another reason why you can't just borrow random recipes, you're not operating in a contextless environment).

Customers have offered me their recipes. A few are simple and make sense, and we've incorporated them into our menu. Most are fussy, complicated, and I have to ask them where I'm supposed to store the additional eight ingredients that go into making their ideal drink.

Hedge

Food business is about calculating and controlling risk. Many can develop their own recipes. Few can write a menu that reduces risk. For instance, it's unwise to have one menu item with ingredients that aren't found in any other item. What if this item doesn't sell? It's too risky. Another example is how we use yams. We get a good price on them because we purchase them in bulk. To ensure that they don't rot, we have to use them quickly. So we offer baked yams. Baked yams that don't sell within a day and refrigerated and used in protein shakes (Power Meal). Yam is also used to make yam chips. We do something similar with kale. Fresh batch we use for salads and smoothies. Older batch is used for kale chips. We give ourselves the option to use collard greens in green smoothies just in case the price of kale quadruples (it happens). Making a menu isn't like making a music mix of one's favorite songs. It's figuring out ways to minimize risk and waste.

Don't hire anyone

I learned this one the hard way. If you've never worked in the food industry and don't have a network from which you can hire good employees, work the job on your own. It'll help you build mental toughness and patience and get you accustomed to working long hours. You'll be surprised how productive you can be when you work on your mental muscles. Hire only after you've developed workflow processes you're satisfied with and are consistently profitable. Don't hire so you can be lazy. Hire only so you can expand hours and/or devote energy to other aspects of business.

Be cautious when hiring. As Anthony Bourdain has said over and over again, the food industry isn't for most people. You're going to lose a lot of money hiring employees who produce negative value (produce value less than what they're paid).

Don't be afraid to piss off customers

If you're not pissing people off, then there's something wrong with you and your business. You're scared and lack passion. Don't give customers a reason to look down at you, be dignified. And you shouldn't be in this business if your goal is to be popular. Be in it because your convictions are deep and you believe it's your higher calling to improve the world, to change the way people eat and think about food.

Burn your business textbooks

Most of the ideas in business textbooks are asinine. Like focus groups and marketing research. As Steve Jobs put it, "how are people supposed to know whether they like something if they've never seen anything like it?" Start-ups require recklessness, instinct, adaptability, tenacity, and flexibility, not book

learning.

CHAPTER THIRTY FIVE -- ETIQUETTE

DEFINITIONS

Good etiquette: rules of conduct to maximize efficiency and to keep costs down while benefiting the greater good.

Bad etiquette: rules of conduct that allows one to covertly spotlight one's narcissistic needs (eg. recognition as world's nicest person) at the expense of the greater good.

PHONE

If placing an order:

- Don't ask how we're doing. You don't see what's going on on our end so don't waste time.
- Place your order in as few words as possible to minimize communication errors. Wait for us to repeat order back to you. If correct, let us know it's correct. If incorrect, start over and repeat process.

If you want to speak to manager or owner

- Don't ask how we're doing. You don't see what's going on on our end so don't waste time with small talk.
- Identify yourself and the purpose of your call immediately, before you ask to speak to someone, and especially before you start trying to sell us this and that.

*Failure to follow etiquette means we'll hang up on you.

* It's bad manners to ask how someone is doing if you don't care how they're doing.

ORDERING

- There are NO lines. Don't even think about starting one, the space isn't designed for that.
- Take your time to decide, but CALL OUT your order the MOMENT you decide, even if you don't see anyone or all employees look busy. Unlike most everyone else in your life, we're always listening to you, even when we're busy.
- Wait for someone to confirm your order. Once confirmed, chill/hangout/relax. Lots of cool toys for you to play with while waiting for order.
- You DON'T need to SHOUT out your order unless the blenders are on or you're calling out your order from like the bathroom or the dance studio. Just be loud enough that someone will hear you.
- DON'T start asking other customers if they were there first. Or if they'd like to go ahead of you — especially when it's clear they're not ready to order — even though you're ready to order. Such behavior won't get you into the Kingdom of Heaven, God will go Sodom and Gomorrah on those who pull that kind of shit because it's an example of covert narcissism.

Showing Gratitude

- Don't overdo it, less is more. One "thank you" per transaction, not the 3-5 we typically hear. Politeness grandstanding doesn't make one a better person, often it's a sign of social ineptitude and vileness of character.
- "Please" is unnecessary. I get it, some of you are asking us for a favor, to give you what you want (which we don't have to do). But this is still a transactional exchange, where it's given that we'll be taking

your money in exchange for product and service. Also, "please" adds a layer of formality that's unnecessary in a business that tries to be as informal as possible.
- "Polite" fillers like "when you get a chance," or "if you don't mind," aren't just meaningless phrases, they increase chance of misunderstanding. The more you say, the higher the chance for misunderstanding. Be concise, say only what needs to be said.

Rude Behavior

Below are examples of common rude behavior:

- Asking "how are you?" while walking away from the person you're asking the question. Don't ask questions you don't mean to ask. Just say "hi" if that's all you mean to say.
- Asking questions and then not listening to someone's response because you assume you know how they will respond .
- Treating others as you want to be treated. Not everyone wants to be treated as you want to be treated.

* Failure to follow etiquette means no service or the worst service you'll ever experience. So bad that you'll remember it on your deathbed.

*Those who follow etiquette get perks, like free chips and brownies, and get the best service they'll ever experience in the whole_wide_world.

PART V -- NUTS AND BOLTS

Hatred is gained as much by good works as by evil.
-- Machiavelli

CHAPTER THIRTY SIX -- HOW TO RUN A JUICE BAR

Don't try to beat the competition by making the best product
Instead, pick a price point and make the best product for that price point. If you ask me which juice bar has the best salads, I'll pick Heartbeet Cafe. But I don't try to make a salad similar to theirs because theirs costs $15, while mine costs $6. My customers show up 3-5 times a week, theirs show up once or twice a month.

The process is the business
Amateurs think about recipes, professionals care about processes. Focus on process, not recipes. When a process breaks down, everything goes to shit. Create processes that minimize mistakes and speed up delivery time. Remove anyone, including customers, who repeatedly fucks up the process. Letting a process break down is much deadlier to a business than pissing off a few customers.

Base recipes on process
Recipes should be based on, for instance, how long you want people to wait for something, never on what makes it seem fancy to customers. Complicated recipes means longer wait time and more mistakes so keep it simple. Less is more and less tastes the best.

Choose ingredients based on infrastructure and price stability

Again, restaurants don't begin with recipes. They begin with your ability to work with the space and utilities infrastructure to develop recipes unique to your situation. Ingredients you choose to use should be based on the context you're working in: from the price stability and hardiness of an ingredient to the equipment you have. Use ingredients in as many recipes as possible so you can purchase them at a volume discount and hedge against low sales of certain items. For instance, we use beets in multiple drinks, a salad, and as chips. That allows us to buy beets at a much lower price point than if we only used it in a salad. The Nasty Shit smoothie is possible not because it sells well — it doesn't, its purpose on the menu is to brand us as serious about veggies – but because its ingredients are used in our best selling drinks.

Choose your customers
Customers don't choose you, you choose them. This will make you more proactive in getting to know your customers — their fears and dreams — and make work more enjoyable. When you host a party at your home, would you prefer to choose whom to invite or do you let random people in? Costco doesn't let everyone in. The best night clubs let few people in.

We chose the "Redneck Juice Bar" brand because juice bars, like yoga studios, are gendered feminine and men were refusing to come in. So we masculinized the juice bar so much so that 50 percent of our customers are now men, especially working class men. And many of them are drinking kale smoothies and eating their veggies, they tip well, are respectful, they're just fun to serve and be around. To get their business, we had to piss off a lot of pompous and condescending customers, customers you and your employees shouldn't have to deal with anyway.

CHAPTER THIRTY SEVEN -- USE OF MUSIC

People comment on the "unusual" and "daring" music that's played at Alive Juice Bar. It's eclectic, from bossa nova to gangsta rap, from No-Wave punk to bubble gum pop, from acid jazz to redneck rock. And it's music from around the world. There are also a lot of songs about death.

The music choices are deliberate, rarely random. They're meant to communicate to customers an approach to life and a set of values. Sometimes they're used to trigger childhood memories in customers, esp. those between 40-60, our core demographic audience, so their experience at Alive is memorable. The unfamiliar music reflects our goal, which is to introduce and make accessible to customers food they're not familiar with. Music that's "shocking" (offensive to some) or "unusual" is used to ensure that customers are *present* and engaged with the experience of being at Alive Juice Bar, and to help them become comfortable with being uncomfortable. Our music also lets customers know that they've entered a juice bar that's a critique of the safe and repetitive music played in suburban establishments.

We also use the music to help set a work rhythm, to make sure everyone on the floor is following the same beat. Listen to the sound of work at Alive Juice Bar. It's jarring when the sound and rhythm of work is off (listen to the sound of the blenders, the juicer, the shuffling of feet, the pouring of ice). When the sound of work is right, when everyone is in rhythm with each other, customers feel tranquil, at ease, even when it's busy and noisy. Customers aren't just paying for a product, they're paying for a performance.

The wide range of music helps train our employees to become cosmopolitan cross-generational cultural omnivores so they can gain a wider perspective of and appreciation for the world. The music provides callow employees an opportunity to better understand customers from other generations, nations, and socio-economic backgrounds. We typically add "offensive" music to each mix to make sure employees are *present* — that's why you'll see them running to change the music when a child or someone they think will be offended enters. We make sure employees' senses are always turned on.

There's a lot of contrast between one song and another. For instance, we'll go from gangsta rap such as Tupac's taunting, angry and expletive filled "Hit Em Up" to country pop such as Taylor Swift's teenage love song "You Belong With Me." The sharp contrasts, we hope, helps customers and employees remain *present* while at Alive Juice Bar and teach them how different contrasts produce different effects. (Understanding contrasts is key to making good meals).

The contrasts aren't random. Each mix has a theme and a tendency. We have, for instance, the "suicide mix," that includes music from The Sundays, The Smiths, Violent Femmes, Joy Division. There's the "Suburban Redneck" mix, which includes music from Bon Jovi and Journey. There's "Music for White people who hate being White," "The Naughty Hipster," "Pretentious," "Angry," whatever. Each mix includes easily recognizable mainstream songs (that typically follow obscure songs), obscure songs, and indie/alternative songs that'll be easily recognized by some, not others.

Music is an important part of the performance. Think of your business as a performance. Use music to enhance and inspire the performance.

CHAPTER THIRTY EIGHT -- GUIDELINES

JUICE NAZI SEEKS HEAD OF SECRET POLICE

- Alive Juice Bar is a bullshit and repression free zone
- Sometimes the customer is wrong
- Order what you want, even if you can't pay for it
- You can start a tab, pay it off at your convenience
- A customer who is full of shit deserves to be treated like shit
- If you can't pay off your tab because you lost your job, we'll take care of it.
- We'll name a drink after you if you can't pay off your tab because of strip-club habit
- We'll name a drink after you if you're an asshole
- We have the right to refuse service to assholes
- It's OK to stare at employee's ass. Just be discreet about it. Enjoy!
- Employees are allowed to fight with customers
- One of the employees knows kung fu. Do you really want to guess the one?
- Be kind, not nice. Let us know when something's not to your liking and we'll fix it for you.
- Smile, God is watching you!

One of them might know kung fu. So don't fuck with them.

One of these bitches wouldn't follow Guidelines and tried to start a line because she thought it the polite thing to do.

Well, she was wrong. So she turned into a snowman with a small penis.

ABOUT THE AUTHOR

Andrew An Ho

Author started Alive Juice Bar in 2010. He tried to rename it Redneck Juice Bar in 2015 but the landlord wouldn't allow it. He hates acai bowls and wants to buy one so he can throw it at someone.

PRAISE FOR AUTHOR

"Rude. Rude rude rude…:

"He really is a Pig!"

"Quite possibly the worst call in experience in my entire life."

"Okay, so this place is completely insane. Sorry, Andrew, but you are batshit crazy."

"I'd give no star if I could. The Check in offer is rude & crude & just plain inappropriate for a business that deals with the public."

"Things can get dysfunctional at times…"

"I like going to Alive Juice Bar, despite the music, the sound of the blenders, and the frequency of customer ejections."

"…this was the most psychotic experience I've ever had."

"THE WORST PLACE EVER. He said he can't serve us because he doesn't like us!"

"It is true that the service is a tad bit abrasive, and takes getting used to just like the food."

"The owner is…not a lot of "warm & fuzzy…"

"...pretentious prick told me to go to Jamba Juice."

"This place is...super weird."

"I HATE this place so much my pussy hair is turning gray."

"It's infuriating to see these kind of things taking place."

"This place is an oasis from our decayed society – a safe haven for misanthropists so to speak."

"So... the owner claims to not serve assholes, but he was kinda acting like one behind the counter."

"Owner was telling new employee to call customers 'motherfucker'."

"This place isn't for everyone. I think that's their point."

"The awful owner told my son that the snowman will bite off his penis...he has nightmares now!"

"...this place is strange. I had a smoothie which was fine, but yea, the customer service is terrible."

"Although the juice is fine, among at least 5 different people that I interacted only one of them was actually nice. They rest were more like "Why are you here". Especially once I was about to leave because when I walked to the counter and gave them my order, nobody looked at my face and the guy (without making eye contact) said "Just yell it out and we'll make it ready" with a frustrated facial expression followed by a sigh."

"My review can't even begin to explain what a jerk this guy is – I can't believe anyone goes back.."

"I'm more mad I didn't get that monkey face middle finger thing."

- YELP REVIEWS

Made in the USA
Columbia, SC
15 August 2020